A Year in Rhyme

FRANCES HENDERSON

PAGE PUBLISHING, INC.
New York, NY

First originally published by Page Publishing, Inc. 2016

ISBN 978-1-68409-993-1 (Paperback)
ISBN 978-1-68409-994-8 (Digital)

Printed in the United States of America

Compiled for my beloved Granny,
Stephanie Dobbs Alexander.

A Year in Rhyme

I did not set out to write a book. This book came from a challenge I gave myself at the beginning of the year. For several years now, I have read my Bible from cover to cover. I tried reading different translations and paraphrases. I even read one called the Chronological Bible. That one didn't hold my interest long. I felt like I was cheating by not reading every sentence of every book. Anyway, sometimes I would read, close the Bible, and walk away, thinking that I couldn't even remember what I had just read. So I decided to challenge myself and see if I could pay such close attention to what I was reading that I could write a poem about something in that day's reading every day.

That's how *A Year in Rhyme* came to be.

If you don't think you have time to read the full Bible readings required each day to cover the Bible in a year, maybe you could start out by reading the poem for that day. Maybe that poem will so perk your curiosity that you will find yourself turning more and more often to Scripture to see what is behind the thought of that day's poem. Or maybe some of the poems will give you a new perspective on a reading. I hope you get as much out of reading this book as I did in writing it.

> Give thanks to the Lord, call on His name;
> make known among the nations what He has
> done. (Psalm 105:1)

Frances Henderson
2013

Creation
January 1, Genesis 1–3

In the beginning, before time began,
God created the world for man.
He created light and color and sound
And every creature that can be found.

Then God created a garden so fair,
And when He had finished, He placed man there.
God gave him the job of the garden's care,
Then fashioned a woman, his life to share.

The Flood
January 2, Genesis 4–6

This was not just a sprinkle of raindrops
Gently hitting the ground.
No, these were the tears of Almighty God,
Streaming, pouring down.
Why wouldn't mankind listen?
Why couldn't they understand?
Obedience was all He was asking,
Yet He found it in only one man.

The windows of Heaven were opened
And water poured down from on high.
And then the springs of the deep burst forth
Until nothing on earth was left dry.
The waters came together,
From the earth and those from on high,
Until all the earth was covered,
There was only water and sky.

And an ark.

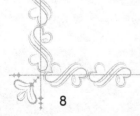

A Rainbow

January 3, Genesis 7–9

When storm clouds roll above you
And skies are dark and gray,
Don't let the gloom distract you
Or steal your joy away.

For God has made a promise
And sealed it with a bow,
A lovely rainbow in the sky
So everyone will know.

Tower of Babel
January 4, Genesis 10–12

When Satan gets a foothold
And guides the thoughts of men,
It always causes trouble,
And soon it leads to sin.
Just ask the men of Babel,
In the Bible long ago.
They sought to build a tower;
To Heaven they would go.

They didn't need God's wisdom,
His guidance, or His love.
They'd simply keep on building till
They reached His home above.
But men can't get to Heaven
By their knowledge or their skill.
It takes the hand of God Himself;
A hand He offers still.

A Tithe: A Tenth

January 5, Genesis 13–15

Abram went to battle
To save his nephew, Lot.
He rescued all the people,
Winning victory on the spot.

When he returned from battle,
He refused the victor's prize.
Instead he gave the praise to God
And gave to Him a tithe.

It may be just a penny,
A nickel, or a dime.
But we should give a tithe—a tenth—
Every single time.

Let God Work His Plan

January 6, Genesis 16–18

Sarah was impatient,
She found it hard to wait.
God had promised her a son,
Why did He hesitate?

Maybe she should help Him
And move this plan along.
And so she sent in Hagar,
But, boy, that move was wrong.

So Hagar had a baby,
And Ishmael was his name.
But life within old Abram's camp
Was never more the same.

If you are ever tempted
To help God work His plan,
Remember, He can do all right
Without your helping hand.

Rescued by Angels
January 7, Genesis 19–21

Lot chose to live in Sodom,
A city steeped in sin.
But when two angels came one day,
He gladly took them in.

The angels gave him warning,
He had to leave or die.
But somehow Lot resisted
And failed to heed their cry.

At last the angels took him,
And holding to his hand,
They led him and his family out
As fire fell on the land.

A Wife for Isaac
January 8, Genesis 22–24

Abraham was growing old and wanted to provide
For his young son Isaac a fit and proper bride.

And so he sent his servant, a wise and honest man,
Back to his home country with a carefully thought-out plan.

He took rich gifts to please her and prayed God lead the way.
And that's how fair Rebekah came to be a bride that day.

War in the Womb
January 9, Genesis 25–27

We all know siblings quarrel,
They struggle and compete.
There is jealousy and envy.
There are obstacles to meet.

But did you know that struggle
Can begin within the womb;
When twins are there and have to share
That far-too-little room?

That happened to Rebekah
When two nations would begin
By her sons Esau and Jacob
As they struggled from within.

Work for a Bride
January 10, Genesis 28–30

We all love good romances,
The hearts and flowers kind.
And here we have a story
Like no other you will find.

Jacob worked for seven years
To wed his Rachel sweet,
Just to find that Laban was
A liar and a cheat.

When sunrise came next morning,
To Jacob's great surprise,
He found that he was looking
Into Leah's lovely eyes.

But Jacob was no quitter,
His love was strong and true.
He worked another seven years
And wed his Rachel too.

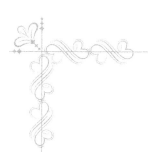

Wrestle with God
January 11, Genesis 31–33

Jacob wrestled with the thought
Behind his mother's plan
To steal his brother's blessing,
Esau was a hairy man.

Years later, Jacob wrestled
And fought a war of words,
When Laban came against him
To claim his flocks and herds.

But in his greatest battle,
Jacob wrestled through the night
And found it was the Lord Himself
With whom he had the fight.

The Lord gave him a blessing
And then He changed his name;
And never, ever after
Was Jacob quite the same.

Angry Retaliation of Brothers

January 12, Genesis 34–36

Jacob had a daughter and Dinah was her name.
A man named Shechem raped her, which
brought on her great shame.
Though Shechem really loved her and asked if they could wed,
Dinah's brothers tricked him and lied to him instead.
They said the two could marry if their men were circumcised,
But then they killed them one and all,
taking plunder as their prize.

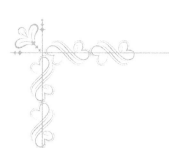

Joseph's Coat
January 13, Genesis 37–39

When Joseph was a little boy, he loved to dream and plan
Of all the things that he would do when he became a man.
But Joseph's many brothers were jealous as could be,
For he was Daddy's favorite and that was plain to see.

Jacob was a good man, but maybe not too wise,
For he had made a special coat that truly was a prize.
But it was made for Joseph and so resentment grew.
The lovely coat turned out to show what jealousy can do.

From Prison to Power

January 14, Genesis 40–42

Poor Joseph was in prison
Though he had done no wrong.
And even there God used him
As his faith and love stayed strong.

Two men were placed in prison
Where they each had troubling dreams.
But Joseph gave their meanings
And he was right, it seems.

It happened two years later
That Pharaoh heard the tale.
He quickly sent for Joseph
To explain his dream as well.

Joseph gave the answer
And gave God all the praise.
They made him Pharaoh's right hand man
All his remaining days.

Family Reunion
January 15, Genesis 43–45

When we think about family reunions,
With uncles and cousins galore,
We think about picnics with chicken
And veggies and pies and much more.

But at one famous family reunion
(In the Bible the story is told)
The reunion was simply twelve brothers
And a tale of intrigue that unfolds.

Egyptians in Bondage
January 16, Genesis 46–48

The Egyptian people were hungry.
The famine was severe.
They gave Joseph all their money,
But their crops failed year after year.

When all their pockets were empty,
They traded their livestock away.
And still the famine lingered
Till they had nothing to pay.

Last of all, they sold their land
And pledged themselves to be
In bondage unto Pharaoh
To save their families.

Death of a Father

January 17, Genesis 49–50

It hurts to lose a loved one
No matter who they are.
But when it is a parent,
The grief is worse by far.

Jacob's life was ending.
He knew that death was near;
And so he called for all his sons
And gave each a blessing clear.

One hundred forty seven years
And then death came his way;
And even Egypt mourned his loss
For seventy long days.

Why Me, Lord?

January 18, Exodus 1–4

Have you ever asked the question:
"Why me, Lord? Why me?"
It's usually when we're hurting
And a reason we can't see.
We question God's great kindness,
His wisdom and His love.
We feel that we're mistreated
So we question God above.

But what about old Moses?
He asked that question too.
Except he wasn't hurting.
God gave him a job to do.
He offered up excuses
And gave God reasons why,
But God said simply, "Do it!
I'll be with you if you try."

The Plagues Begin
January 19, Exodus 5–7

Pharaoh was an evil man and stubborn as could be.
So he ignored the warning to set God's people free.

At first God sent a sample—a preview you might say—
Of what the future held for him if he did not obey.

Aaron took the rod he held and threw it to the ground.
It turned into a serpent, slithering around.

But Pharaoh wasn't shaken, he thought it just a show.
And then the waters turned to blood,
with nine more plagues to go.

Plagues in Egypt Continue
January 20, Exodus 8–10

Frogs came from the water and covered all the ground.
Then the dust turned into gnats; relief could not be found.

Flies became the problem when they swarmed across the land.
Except in Goshen, which the Lord covered with His hand.

Next, Egyptian livestock quickly sickened and then died.
And boils broke out on people, who in pain and anguish cried.

The plague that numbered seven that
continued God's great wrath
Was a record-breaking hailstorm killing all within its path.

Then God sent down a darkness as thick as it could be;
A blanket of black so heavy that no one in Egypt could see.

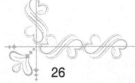

A Plague and a Promise
January 21, Exodus 11–13

The final plague God sent them was the harshest of them all.
The death of every first-born son was the judgment of this call.
The first-born son of Pharaoh and of workers and of slaves.
All through the land of Egypt there was
grief and tears and graves.

But a promise then was given to God's people on that night.
Death's angel would pass over them
and they would be all right.
God gave them clear instructions, what
to eat, and what to wear.
And the Hebrews left their bondage—
what a story they could share.

Red Sea or Sea of Reeds?
January 22, Exodus 14–16

It used to say the *Red Sea*
In every book you read.
But now folks say it should be called
The *Sea of Reeds* instead.
They say the Sea of Reeds is marsh,
With water ankle high.
But that doesn't fit the story.
If you read it, you'll see why.

Scripture says the water
Formed a wall on either side,
And Israelites crossed over
On ground that now had dried.
But when Egyptians followed,
All the horses and the men
Were swallowed as the waters
Flowed back into place again.

Lifted Hands

January 23, Exodus 17–19

God's children fought a battle
And Joshua led the way.
The Amalekites were warriors,
And they struggled with them all day.

Moses stood on the hilltop,
His hands held high in prayer.
The battle seemed to go their way
As long as he stood there.

But Moses's arms grew weary,
His hands began to drop.
And when they did, the battle waned,
The enemy wouldn't stop.

Aaron and Hur to the rescue,
They held his hands up high.
And at sunset the battle was over.
The Lord is my banner, they cried.

The Giving of the Law
January 24, Exodus 20–22

As God led His children forward, He
gave them rules on how to live.
First He gave the Ten Commandments, but
there was so much more to give.

God came down upon the mountain to let His people hear,
But they heard the mighty thunder and
it filled their hearts with fear.

God warned them against idols and told them how to treat
The servants in their households, even those they had to beat.

There were also laws for injuries and property and more.
God gave them careful guidelines for
what the future held in store.

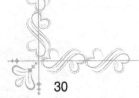

The Law Continues
January 25, Exodus 23–25

Some folks think the Bible is full of "Thou shall not's."
But if you really read it, it says, "Thou shall" a lot.

How many in our world today are stressed beyond belief?
Yet in His Word, God scheduled times to give us great relief.

The seventh day was special, a time of rest for all.
And every seventh year, the land should not be worked at all.

God scheduled celebrations at certain times each year,
When people came together and brought their offerings near.

God knew when we get busy and never stop to rest
Our bodies and our minds slow down
and we can't do our best.

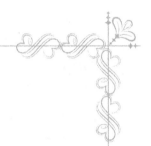

Building a Tabernacle
January 26, Exodus 26–28

The people brought their offerings,
Each one gave generously.
They brought their silver, gold, and bronze,
And cloth made lovingly.

Finely twisted linen made
The curtains which were hung.
With loops of blue and clasps of gold,
Together they were strung.

Pure olive oil was given,
The lamps must not go out.
God gave them clear instructions
So there could be no doubt.

And then they made fine garments
For Aaron and his sons.
The job that they were given
Was not an easy one.

When God Calls
January 27, Exodus 29–31

God chose Aaron and his sons
To serve as Israel's priests.
He gave details of their duties
From the greatest to the least.

Then God called two other men
And gave them talents rare
To work with gold and silver
Crafting items with great care.

God never calls a person
To do a special task,
Until He gives them all they need
To do what He has asked.

The Golden Calf
January 28, Exodus 32–34

Moses went up on the mountain
To receive the Lord's commands.
But the people grew impatient
In this dry and dusty land.

They took their pleas to Aaron.
They wanted idols made.
How quickly they'd forgotten
All the promises they'd made.

Aaron took their earrings
And melted down the gold.
From this he made a calf for them,
A god that they could hold.

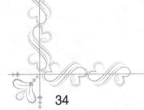

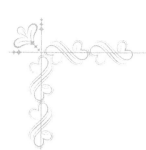

Gifts Were Given

January 29, Exodus 35–37

The plans had all been given.
The time had come to build.
God called for gifts and offerings
And workers who were skilled.

They brought both gold and silver
And scarlet thread and blue,
Onyx stones and other gems
And oil and spices too.

The people's hearts were tender
And gifts were brought galore.
Till Moses finally told them,
Don't bring us any more.

The Work Begins

January 30, Exodus 38–39

The materials were gathered.
Now at last the work could start.
Every single Israelite
Was glad to do his part.

Some wove finest linen
For the curtains which were hung.
And all in all the gold they used,
Weighed just over a ton.

The bronze to make the basin
Came from mirrors melted down.
What a tribute to the ladies.
Such great love is seldom found.

Aaron and his sons were dressed
In garments made with care,
Like an ephod and a breast piece
Trimmed in stones both rich and rare.

Put It All Together

January 31, Exodus 40

The Lord said unto Moses,
Bring it all together now.
And put each piece within its place
Just as I have told you how.

First put up the meeting tent
With the ark set deep within.
And in front you place the curtain
So that folks will not go in.

Every article God mentioned,
Tables, altars, lamps, and tools,
Each was placed with deep precision,
All according to God's rules.

Then a cloud from Heaven covered it,
God's glory filled the day.
Either cloud or fire guided them
As they moved on their way.

Voluntary Offerings
February 1, Leviticus 1–3

God gave clear instructions for each offering they could give.
And Moses taught the people what to do if they would live.

The first was a burnt offering because it was to be
Totally and completely burned for everyone to see.

It was meant to pay the price for sins done every day
And represent devotion to the God who led their way.

A grain offering was next in line, and it was burned in part,
But all the rest was given to the priests right from the start.

A peace offering was next described, and then you may recall,
They were told that they must eat no blood or fat at all.

Required Offerings
February 2, Leviticus 4–6

Some offerings were given
As led by one's own heart.
Others were required by God
With details for each part.

The sin offering was offered
To show God our regret
For sins committed carelessly
Or simply by neglect.

The guilt offering that was required
For liars and for cheats
Included restitution
Plus a 20 percent increase.

Instructions Continue
February 3, Leviticus 7–8

Leviticus is hard to read,
But as we do we see,
How glorious the gift of grace
Christ brought to you and me.

There's no more need to shed the blood
Of animals each day
Or worry that we might have touched
Some unclean thing some way.

We don't need priests to stand before
Our God to intercede.
For Jesus Christ has paid our way.
He's all we'll ever need.

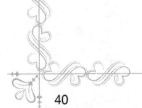

Serious Business

February 4, Leviticus 9–10

Animals were slaughtered
And sacrifices made.
First for Aaron and his sons
Then the people as they prayed.

Aaron blessed the people with
His hands both lifted high.
When the glory of the Lord appeared,
Folks gave a joyful cry.

But two of Aaron's sons that day
Were careless in their tasks.
They offered incense to the Lord
In ways He had not asked.

Fire from God consumed them.
They both died on that day.
A lesson we all need to learn:
To obey is to serve God's way.

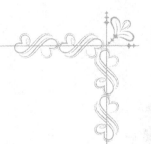

Clean/Unclean
February 5, Leviticus 11–13

This portion of the Scripture is tedious to read.
It's just so full of dos and don'ts we fail to see the need.

Why do you think God gave such rules
of things we could not eat?
When later on, He let men have most any kind of meat.

It's all about obedience. Life really is a test
To see if we'll do our own thing or what God says is best.

Skin Diseases and Mildew

February 6, Leviticus 14–5

God spoke of skin diseases
And mildew in a wall.
He gave them clear instructions
On how to treat them all.

Remember, these were written
A long, long time ago,
And there were many things back then
They simply didn't know.

But if they each would follow
God's rules, then they would find
That they would have a lifestyle
Of the strong and healthy kind.

Day of Atonement
February 7, Leviticus 16–8

The Day of Atonement came just once a year,
And God gave instructions both detailed and clear.
Only the high priest could enter that day
Into the Holy of Holies to pray.

He must carry incense with smoke rising high
To shield him from God, lest he should die.
Atonement was made for the Most Holy Place,
The tent, the altar, and the priest in this case.

There were also two goats brought before the priest.
One was slaughtered, the other released.
The sacrifice meant God forgave them that day,
And the "scapegoat" carried their guilt away.

Rules to Live By

February 8, Leviticus 19–21

The Lord spoke unto Moses
And told him he must give
A list of regulations
By which they all should live.

God told them to be Holy;
A people set apart;
A people who would follow Him
With pure, obedient hearts.

And then God gave a list of things
That they were not to do
To help them live these holy lives
Just as He told them to.

Feast Days
February 9, Leviticus 22–23

The Lord gave the children of Israel
Nineteen days each year
To draw aside and do no work,
To worship and draw near.

These were nineteen days in addition
To the Sabbath day each week
For rest and for celebration,
The face of God to seek.

For Passover, one day was given
And it was followed by
Seven days of unleavened bread
To remember the Exodus by.

The Feast of First Fruits was just one day,
The Feast of Weeks just one.
Also the Feast of Trumpets which
Was a day of great joy and good fun.

The Day of Atonement was one day
Of solemn reflection and prayer.
Then seven more days to remember
All of God's guidance and care.

The Year of Jubilee

February 10, Leviticus 24–25

Each fiftieth year, they must proclaim
A jubilee to praise God's name.
They could not sow nor could they reap.
The land must rest—a Sabbath sleep.

A man who sold his property
Could have it back at Jubilee.
And any slave a man had bought
Must be set free as God's Word taught.

The Importance of Obedience
February 11, Leviticus 26–27

Men were not left in question
About God's Holy will.
He spelled it out quite clearly
And it will guide us still.

The bottom-line is to obey,
A daily choice it seems.
For which He promised blessings sure
Beyond our wildest dreams.

But if we choose to go our way,
The judgment He will send
Will rob our lives of peace and joy,
Our fear will have no end.

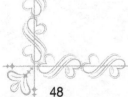

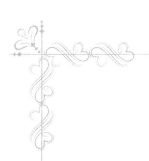

The First Census
February 12, Numbers 1–2

There was a census taken
Of all the strong, young men
Twenty years or older
And fit to fight and win.

Tribal men were chosen
With names too hard to say,
And Moses wrote the numbers
They brought to him that day.

The Levites were not counted,
Their job was not to fight.
They'd tend the Tabernacle
And guard it day and night.

The Levites Chosen

February 13, Numbers 3–4

God chose the tribe of Levi
To be His very own,
In place of every first born male,
To serve as they were shown.

The Levites then were given
A list of jobs to do.
Each with a special duty
That he must carry through.

Each time the tent of meeting
Must move from place to place,
Each person knew what he must do
And quickly set the pace.

Because of this, the moving
Was organized and fast,
While Aaron and his sons stood watch
From first job to the last.

Unfaithful Wife

February 14, Numbers 5–6

I wonder what old Moses
Would have to say today
About the way most folks ignore
What Scripture has to say.

The test within this Scripture
Is hard to understand.
It tells of jealous feelings
That come upon a man.

Then drinking bitter water
Would bring about the truth.
The woman had no option,
God, Himself, would give the proof.

Dedication of the Tabernacle
February 15, Numbers 7

The people worked together, and at last the job was done.
The Tabernacle stood complete before them in the sun.
And Moses called the tribes to bring their offerings one by one.

Moses consecrated it, each piece as God had said,
And now t'was time to dedicate it for the work ahead.
One tribe brought their offering each day just as God led.

There were silver plates and silver bowls
and dishes of pure gold;
Fine flour and oil and rich incense and animals one year old.
Each tribe brought an equal gift, and soon they met their goal.

When all the gifts were given, and Moses went inside,
He heard the mighty voice of God calling him aside.
From there God spoke to Moses, words
to bolster and to guide.

Cloud by Day
February 16, Numbers 8–9

As the Israelites traveled along their way,
A pillar of cloud traveled with them by day.
When the day was over and the sun went down,
The pillar became a fire all around.

When God lifted the cloud from above the tent,
The Israelites knew what that message meant.
They were to travel and follow the cloud,
And they weren't to stop until God allowed.

When the cloud stopped before them and stood in place,
The Israelites camped with each clan in its space.
By day or by night, when the cloud lifted high,
The Israelites traveled and didn't ask why.

Quail

February 17, Numbers 10–11

The children of Israel quickly forgot
How life was as Egyptian slaves.
They complained to the Lord of their hardships
And many were sent to their graves.

They cried out for fish and for melons,
For cucumbers, garlic, and leeks.
They complained of the boredom of manna,
So God sent them meat for four weeks.

God sent a wind that drove quail from the sea
Till they covered the camp all around.
But the anger of God was aroused by their greed
And a plague cut many folks down.

Leprosy for Miriam
February 18, Numbers 12–13

Miriam grew jealous of the power Moses had.
She complained and criticized and acted very bad.
God first explained how special His ties to Moses were,
And then He sent down leprosy as punishment on her.
But Moses fell upon his face and cried to God above,
"Lord, please forgive and quickly heal this sister that I love."

Ten against Two
February 19, Numbers 14–15

Twelve spies went into Canaan,
As Moses said they should.
And everywhere they looked they found
The land was very good.

But ten of them grew frightened,
The people were so tall.
They called themselves grasshoppers
Because they felt so small.

When they returned with their report,
They scared the people so,
They cried to God and criticized
And simply wouldn't go.

But Joshua and Caleb
Were faithful men and true.
They trusted in God's promises
And knew He'd see them through.

Korah
February 20, Numbers 16–18

First a man named Korah
Led a group of men
In criticizing Moses—
He led them into sin.

God was very angry,
But Moses fell face down
And pleaded for God's mercy,
Laying prostrate on the ground.

Moses warned the people
To move from Korah's side.
Then the ground beneath him opened.
He was swallowed up and died.

Trouble at Kadesh
February 21, Numbers 19–20

The Israelites camped at Kadesh
And laid Miriam to rest.
Then again they started grumbling,
And they put God to the test.

But this time Moses failed them,
He didn't intercede.
In fact, he was so angry
He did a sinful deed.

The people wanted water.
God said, "Speak to the rock."
But Moses struck the rock instead
And gave folks quite a shock.

The sad part was for Moses,
His judgment from God's hand.
He was not allowed to go
Into the Promised Land.

Snakes and a Talking Donkey

February 22, Numbers 21–22

Their travels through the desert covered many weary miles,
And lack of food and water was just part of all their trials.
One day, the Lord sent poisonous
snakes and many people died.
But God sent them a remedy when people wept and cried.

Later in their journey, there is a story told
About a little donkey who spoke up loud and bold.
And even more amazing, the man who owned the beast,
Answered him and didn't seem surprised in the least.

Balak and Balaam
February 23, Numbers 23–25

Balak sent for Balaam to curse the Israelites.
He felt that was the only way that he could win the fight.

Balaam was a sorcerer—one called upon to curse.
But God stepped in and caused him to make the matter worse.

God didn't need a sorcerer to see His will was done.
But he was there at Balak's will, so God said, "He's the one."

Seven altars had been built and Balaam stepped ahead,
But God turned every curse around
and blessed the men instead.

A New Leader Chosen

February 24, Numbers 26–27

The time had come for Moses to leave this world behind.
But first he asked the Lord above to help the people find
Someone who could take his place, a leader strong and true.
One who'd heed God's every word and always follow through.

Joshua, the son of Nun, was God's immediate choice.
He had the heart and strength to lead
and heed the Father's voice.
For years he'd worked by Moses's side;
he knew the laws' demands,
And he could lead them as they went into the Promised Land.

Sacrifices and Holidays
February 25, Numbers 28–29

Old Moses called the people to remind them what to do;
Of all the offerings they should give each
day the whole year through.
Each animal was listed by number and by kind,
And fine flour mixed with olive oil,
the best that they could find.
Along with sacrifices, he scheduled special days
Of feast and celebration for worship and for praise.
Each had a special meaning, just like our holidays,
And each was meant to draw them near
to God to learn His ways.

Midianite Battle

February 26, Numbers 30–31

Israel went to battle
Against the Midianites.
God gave them the victory
After quite a fight.

There were five kings of Midian,
Their names too hard to say.
All five went into battle.
All five were killed that day.

And do you remember Balaam,
That funny little man?
He had a talking donkey
And they spoke as man to man.

He too was in the battle.
He too was killed that day.
God's enemies, take notice.
Don't waste your life that way.

Gadites and Reubenites

February 27, Numbers 32–33

The Gadites and the Reubenites found
land they thought was great
For feeding all their livestock once they
built their pens and gates.

They took their plea to Moses, "Please let us have this land.
Although it's east of Jordan and not in the Promised Land."

At first it angered Moses, this simply wasn't right.
But they assured him they would still help all the others fight.

And so the land was given and promises were made
That they would join their brothers
till their debt was fully paid.

Towns of Refuge
February 28, Numbers 34–36

The Lord gave Moses orders
That he should set aside
Six towns called towns of refuge
Where a man could go to hide
If he had caused another's death
As they worked side by side.

This was God's provision
To give a man the time
To prove that he was innocent
Of planning such a crime.
What happened was an accident
And not a vicious crime.

God also made provision
When someone's guilt was real
That he should forfeit his own life,
His destiny was sealed.
If two or more were witnesses,
There would be no appeal.

A History Lesson
March 1, Deuteronomy 1–2

Sometimes when we are restless
And life seems out of sync,
We need to take some time out
To simply stop and think.

And that is why old Moses
Gave the Israelites one day,
A brief review of history
And how God led the way.

He called to mind the victories
Of battles they had won;
Of manna in the wilderness
And all that God had done.

Sometimes we see our future best
When we review our past.
Remembering ways that God has blessed
With strength for every task.

Warning against Idols
March 2, Deuteronomy 3–4

Moses said to all the people, I want you to recall
When God spoke to you from Horeb as
you stood there, one and all.

Fire blazed upon the mountain, the sky was black as sin.
You heard the words He spoke to you but saw no form within.

So never make an idol in any shape or form.
Don't bow down to the sun or moon
or you will come to harm.

Our God is a jealous God; He warned us from the start.
He demands our full allegiance from a pure and humble heart.

Pass It On

March 3, Deuteronomy 5–7

Moses told the people the laws and the commands
Which God Himself had given and placed within his hand.

He cautioned them to always hold them close to heart
And teach them to their children right from the very start.

At home or work or even bed, they should always share
And write them on their door posts
so all would see them there.

The same is true for us today; our children need to know
The mighty acts of God above and how He loves us so.

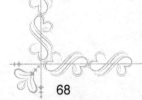

Two Sets of Tablets

March 4, Deuteronomy 8–10

Moses went up on the mountain to
receive the Lord's commands.
God wrote them on stone tablets and
placed them in his hands.
Moses fasted on the mountain forty days and forty nights.
When he came back to the people, he
was met with quite a sight.

For the people made an idol, a calf of purest gold,
And now they laughed and danced around
in actions crude and bold.
Moses let his temper get the best of him that day,
And in a fit of anger, he cast the stones away.

They broke in many pieces, and Moses fell face down
To fast and pray and intercede, lest
God might strike them down.
Then right back up the mountain, Moses
went at God's command,
For a second set of tablets, rules of life for fallen man.

Blessings Versus Curses

March 5, Deuteronomy 11–13

God's promises to Israel were strong and they were true.
But it was up to each of them to heed and follow through.
God promised them great blessings—a
promise they could claim
By living in obedience and worship of His name.
But there were also curses, as strong and true and sure,
If Israel turned away from God, whose laws are just and pure.

Appoint Judges
March 6, Deuteronomy 14–16

The book of Deuteronomy
Is full of dos and don'ts.
It gives us clear directions
As to what our Savior wants.

And in these regulations,
God gave a clear command
That there should be *just* judges
To rule throughout the land.

These men were to be men of God
Who never took a bribe,
And they were to be chosen
From each and every tribe.

If only men would follow
God's just and righteous ways,
God would walk beside them
And bless them all their days.

Military Service
March 7, Deuteronomy 17–20

When it was time for battle,
God laid down some laws
Of men who shouldn't go to war
No matter what the cause.

First, God said that any man
Who recently had built
His family a brand-new home,
Stay there and feel no guilt.

Next, God said that someone
About to take a bride
Should stay at home and marry her
Lest in the war he died.

And finally, God set aside
All those who felt afraid
Lest that fear spread and battle plans
Fall into disarray.

Punishment for Rebellion
March 8, Deuteronomy 21–23

A law that may seem strange to us
That came from God on high
Was if a son did not obey
That son must surely die.

A stubborn and rebellious heart
That spurned a parent's love
Must first be judged and then be stoned,
So said our God above.

As always, when God gives a word
That seems to us unkind,
This too was meant to make men think
Before they crossed that line.

Curses on Mount Ebal
March 9, Deuteronomy 24–27

When you cross the Jordan River and come into the land
The Lord your God has given, then you must go and stand
Before the altar built upon Mount Ebal, close at hand.

Then God gave to the Israelites a lengthy list of facts
Of things that would bring curses if
they took part in such acts.
Things that left them open to the enemy's attacks.

And as each curse was given, the people said, "Amen."
A word which meant "so be it" and signified that men
Agreed they heard and understood such judgment for their sin.

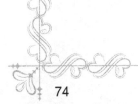

Blessings "If"
March 10, Deuteronomy 28

God offers many promises
Of blessings He will give
Of health and crops and livestock
And land on which to live.

He promised rest from enemies
And peace throughout our days,
But in return He asked of us
To follow in His way.

As you read in your Bible,
Don't skip or overlook
How many times that little word
Of *if* is in the Book.

"If you fully obey the Lord,"
And "If you keep the commands."
"If you pay attention"
You'll be blessed on every hand.

You may not grow wealthy,
Not all blessings come as gold,
But you will live a blessed life
Of joy and peace untold.

Moses's Last Warning

March 11, Deuteronomy 29–31

Moses was an old man of one hundred twenty years
When again he faced the people and
addressed their many fears.
He knew they'd soon be crossing into the Promised Land,
But he would not be leading them, his death was close at hand.

He warned of their rebellion, their tendency to sin,
And then he named the curses that God would surely send.
With life and death before them, they had to make a choice;
Continue on their downward path or listen to God's voice.

Death of Moses
March 12, Deuteronomy 32–34

Moses knew his days were numbered
Even though he still felt strong,
So he spoke of Israel's history
And he wrote it in a song.

Then he called for all the Israelites,
And as the people came,
He gave a special blessing
As he called each tribe by name.

Then Moses climbed Mount Nebo,
And from there God let him see
All the land God promised
Clear to the western sea.

Then Moses's heart was satisfied,
And he drew his final breath.
And all of Israel mourned and wept
In grief for Moses's death.

A Scarlet Cord

March 13, Joshua 1–3

The Lord commanded Joshua that he was now to lead
The people over Jordan, for the land was theirs indeed.

God made a special promise to Joshua that day
That He would not forsake him, as he bravely led the way.

So spies were sent to Jericho, and Rahab hid them there.
And in return, they promised her safety in their care.

She hung a cord of scarlet to let all Israel see
That she had saved the spies they sent,
now they must keep her free.

Memorial Stones
March 14, Joshua 4–6

When the Israelites came to the Jordan
To enter the Promised Land,
They stood on the banks of the river
Awaiting Joshua's command.

First were the priests who carried
The Ark to lead the way.
And when their feet touched the water,
It stopped flowing right away.

So Joshua told twelve leaders
To gather up one stone each
To serve as a stone of remembrance
And a tool with which they could teach.

They carried them over the Jordan
And set them together there
To remind their children in days to come
Of God's miraculous care.

Achan's Sin

March 15, Joshua 7–8

Greed will cause you trouble
Every single time.
You never really profit
When you live a life of crime.

Just ask the man named Achan,
Whose greed led him to sin.
He stole some things, then dug a hole,
And buried them within.

He caused the wrath of God to fall
Upon the Israelites,
And when they went to war again,
They quickly lost the fight.

Today we coddle criminals
With phones and TV sets.
But Achan's family had to die
To cover Achan's debt.

The Sun Stood Still

March 16, Joshua 9–10

Joshua led God's people
To claim the Promised Land.
And everywhere they went,
They followed God's command.

So one day, Joshua asked God
To make the sun stand still;
To give them time to end the fight
In following God's will.

And so the sun stood still that day
In the middle of the sky
Because the Lord had listened
And honored Joshua's cry.

Defeated Kings
March 17, Joshua 11–13

Many kings joined forces
Against the Israelites.
But God encouraged Joshua
That he would win the fight.
The battles raged for seven years,
And when the job was done,
The foreign kings who died in war
Numbered thirty-one.

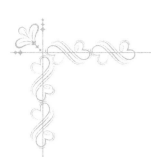

Caleb

March 18, Joshua 14–16

You remember Caleb,
His faith was rich and strong.
He tried to get the Israelites
To trust God all along.
He went to spy out Canaan
With eleven other men
But only one agreed with him
That they could really win.
Now forty-five years later,
As Caleb knew he would,
Joshua awarded him
The land on which he stood.

Five Daughters
March 19, Joshua 17–19

There was a man who had a name
That's very hard to say.
They called his name Zelophehad,
And when he passed away,
He had no sons—just daughters—
Five of them in all.
But way back then, a daughter
Didn't count for much at all.

But these five girls were clever
And together took a stand.
So they received inheritance
By God's direct command.
Alongside all their uncles,
These sisters had a share,
Which set a brand-new precedent.
T'was really only fair.

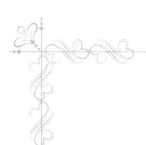

Special Cities
March 20, Joshua 20–21

There were two special kinds of cities
The Israelites set aside.
One was the cities of refuge
Where accused men could go to hide.
The other was towns for the Levites—
Of these there were forty-eight—
With the pasture lands around them
To care for their flocks, which were great.
These cities were God's provision
To help keep the laws of the land,
And His blessing upon the Levites
Who served at His command.

Joshua's Farewell

March 21, Joshua 22–24

Joshua was growing old,
Yet there was work to do.
So he called for the leaders
To warn them to stay true.
God kept His every promise
To give to you this land,
But if you turn away from Him
This nation will not stand.

Then speaking very briefly,
Joshua gave a review
Of how God called and blessed them
And all they had come through.
Now fear the Lord and serve Him,
Was Joshua's command.
And then he made a statement
That typified his stand:

"As for me and my house, we will serve the Lord."

Why Judges?
March 22, Judges 1–2

Joshua died at one hundred and ten, and
his whole generation soon fell.
Then others grew up, but they turned away,
and served other gods as well.
God had kept all of His promises, and
given them land of their own.
But they failed to destroy all their neighbors,
And seeds of rebellion were sown.

Then in words that should strike fear and terror,
In His anger, the Lord "sold them out."

His "hand was against them in battle." No
longer was victory their shout.
But again, the Lord in His kindness, stepped in to save the day.
He sent a series of judges to lead them back to His way.

Deborah and Jael
March 23, Judges 3–5

Deborah was a prophetess and Israel's judge as well.
Her story is a strange one and includes the woman, Jael.

Deborah called for Barak to lead them in the fight
Against a man named Sisera, but Barak saw their might.

"I will not go to battle unless you lead the way."
So Deborah did go with him to fight the war that day.

Now Israel was winning, so Sisera turned and fled.
He sought escape in Jael's tent, but she took his life instead.

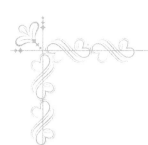

Gideon's Fleece
March 24, Judges 6–7

Israel had sinned again and turned from God's commands.
So the Midianites and the Amalekites were ravaging the land.

Then Gideon saw an angel, who gave him a command,
I'm sending you to save your home out of Midian's hands.

Now Gideon was willing but felt he was too small.
So he asked for a favor—a test you may recall.

He laid a fleece upon the ground, and
when the morning came,
The fleece was wet, the ground was dry, instead of all the same.

One more time he tried it. This time the fleece was dry.
But all around, the ground was wet. This was a battle cry.

Decisions—Wise and Foolish

March 25, Judges 8–9

God gave unto Gideon
Great victories at war.
And as the people bragged on him,
His fame spread near and far.

At first, old Gideon was wise
And gave God all the glory.
But he made a golden ephod
And that was another story.

How wise he was to tell them
He would not be their king.
But then his heart was led astray
By a stupid golden "thing."

Jephthah
March 26, Judges 10–11

The story that's told about Jephthah is
as strange as any you'll hear.
His whole life was marked with heartbreak
and the reasons were usually clear.

It started when he was a young man and
his brothers drove him away.
He was born of a prostitute mother. It was
her sin, but they made him pay.

At one point, he led in battle and it seemed like a brighter day.
But when God gave Jephthah the victory,
a foolish vow caused him dismay.

For Jephthah made a promise without
really thinking it through.
"Whatever meets me coming from
home, Lord, I will give to you."

Jephthah was surely thinking of a goat or a calf or a sheep.
Instead, it was his only daughter. But
the promise he had to keep.

A Riddle
March 27, Judges 12–14

Everyone knows about Samson,
His story is told at great length.
How he killed a lion barehanded
Due to his incredible strength.

Later he looked at the carcass
And in it honey was found.
So he posed a clever riddle
To the thirty men gathered around.

Unfortunately, there was a wager,
Which the men did not want to lose.
So they threatened his wife for the answer,
And she was forced to choose.

When the men gave Samson the answer,
He understood right away.
The only way they could have known it,
His wife gave the answer away.

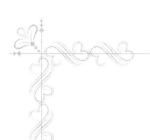

Little Foxes
March 28, Judges 15–17

You know old Samson's story
Of his strength beyond compare.
But some of his encounters
We seldom ever share.

For instance, he once caught foxes,
There were three hundred of them in pairs.
By their tails he tied them together
With torches lit like flares.

He took them to the grain fields,
And once he set them free,
They destroyed the crops and vineyards
And even the olive trees.

Cowardly Levite
March 29, Judges 18–19

The Levites were especially chosen to lead in religious affairs,
But here is the story of one man, whose
actions were sick and unfair.
This Levite had chosen a maiden to
serve as his own concubine,
But as they traveled one evening, they
could not make it home on time.

When they stopped for the night in Gibeah,
some evil men sought him for sex.
But he gave instead the young woman to
these men who were sinful wrecks.
The men raped and beat the maiden. It
lasted all through the night.
She fell dead with her hands on the threshold,
And he found her at morning's first light.

The Benjamites
March 30, Judges 20–21

The Levite of yesterday's story
Cut his concubine's body in parts;
Twelve parts for the twelve tribes of Israel,
And the sight went straight to their hearts.

Eleven tribes of Israel
Against the Benjamites.
And as they came together,
It was really quite a fight.

Twenty-five thousand swordsmen
Of Benjamin were struck down.
And then the Israelites went in
And burned their cities down.

When all the fighting was over
And the smoke cleared out that day,
Six hundred men of Benjamin
Were all who got away.

A Story of Love
March 31, Ruth 1–4

There's a story that's told in the Bible
Of a love both special and rare.
Not love between a man and a woman;
A love of a mother-in-law's care.

We've all heard the jokes and the stories
Of how irritating they can be.
But this mother-in-law turned the tables
And inspired a love rich and free.

But as you read this story,
There's a deeper truth hidden within.
A story of love from our Savior
Who redeems us and saves us from sin.

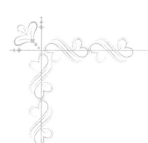

A Son for Hannah
April 1, 1 Samuel 1–3

Hannah was a woman
Called barren in her day.
So she went up to Shiloh
To sacrifice and pray.

As God Almighty listened,
He heard and felt her pain.
He touched her heart with love and peace
That fell like gentle rain.

Then Hannah's prayer was answered,
God sent a baby boy.
And in return, she gave him back
To serve with love and joy.

She called the young boy Samuel,
Which means "God heard" my prayer.
And Samuel lived with Eli,
Serving God with greatest care.

Only One God
April 2, 1 Samuel 4–7

The Philistines had a pagan god, and Dagon was his name.
They built for him a temple and bragged about his fame.
While fighting with the Israelites, the battle went their way.
They took the ark of God from them and carried it away.
They placed it in the temple by Dagon's idol there.
Perhaps they thought it proved their god
was strong beyond compare.

But early the next morning, our God made quite a mark.
For Dagon lay upon the ground, face down before the ark.
The people took old Dagon and put him back in place.
When morning rolled around again, he'd fallen on his face.
But this time it was different, he didn't simply fall.
This time his head and hands broke off. He was no god at all.

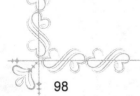

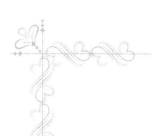

The Cost of a King
April 3, 1 Samuel 8–11

As Samuel was growing old, the people gathered 'round
And whined like little children clustered
on a school playground.

They didn't want another judge, a king was their demand,
Like all the other nations that were found throughout the land.

So God said unto Samuel, give the people what they asked.
But then make sure they understand the cost of such a task.

A king will take your children to fight and work his land.
He'll take your fields and vineyards;
your flocks he will demand.

So you can have a king to lead just like all the rest.
But you will see and count the cost when he takes all your best.

Honey in the Woods
April 4, 1 Samuel 12–14

While Saul was king of Israel,
He made a strange decree
That no one was to eat that day
Till they won victory.

But Jonathan, Saul's precious son,
Did not hear Saul's command,
And in the woods, a honeycomb
Gave him new strength to stand.

Saul set his mind to kill the boy
And send him to his grave.
But all the soldiers took his side
And Jonathan was saved.

Young David
April 5, 1 Samuel 15–16

God sent the prophet Samuel
To Jesse's home one day.
God had rejected Saul as king
For all his prideful ways.

Now Jesse's sons were many—
Eight of them in all—
But he called only seven;
The youngest was too small.

Samuel kept waiting
As each man passed that day.
But God had chosen none of them
And sent them on their way.

At last they called for David,
And much to their surprise,
He was the one anointed
And honored in God's eyes.

David, Goliath, and God
April 6, 1 Samuel 17–18

Here came little David,
A simple shepherd boy.
To the tall and strong Goliath,
He seemed a simple toy.

But David had a secret,
A weapon sure and true.
He knew it was the Lord, Himself
Who would see this battle through.

So David stood before him
With just a sling and stone,
But God directed that small rock
And victory was His own.

Young Jonathan
April 7, 1 Samuel 19–21

Jonathan was quite a man,
No finer friend you'll find.
He was a prince of Israel
Yet he was good and kind.
He was loyal to young David,
The gentle shepherd boy,
And every victory David won
Brought Jonathan great joy.

Now Saul was king of Israel,
And it was in his plan
That when time came for change of rule,
His son would be that man.
But Jonathan was willing
To quietly step aside,
For he knew David was God's choice
So he'd serve by David's side.

Innocent Blood

April 8, 1 Samuel 22–24

Saul had sunk so low in sin he called his fighting men
To strike down all the priests of Nob
though they were free of sin.
The deed was so horrific, the soldiers standing near
Refused to heed his orders, they stood and shook with fear.
But then Doeg the Edomite, who
craved both wealth and fame,
Stepped forward to fulfill the act t'was his great sin and shame.
He killed all eighty-five of them, each one an honored priest.
And then he struck their city and killed eldest to the least.
Now Doeg swung the sword that day
at his hand blood did fall.
But it was Saul who must accept the greatest guilt of all.

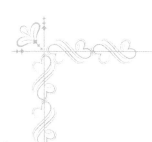

David's Wisdom

April 9, 1 Samuel 25–27

Part of David's wisdom
Was learning how to wait
And let the Lord direct him
About another's fate.

Twice he spared the life of Saul.
Much to his men's dismay.
But Saul was God's anointed;
David chose to wait and pray.

Another life which David spared
Was Nabal—which means "fool."
But Nabal's wife, wise Abigail,
Stepped in and kept things cool.

If David had not listened
To Abigail that day,
He would have rendered vengeance.
God had a better way.

Saul's Choices
April 10, 1 Samuel 28–31

Saul never wanted to be king, he made his feelings clear.
When Samuel came to crown him, he hid among the gear.

Once, before a battle, when Samuel ran late,
Saul burned up the sacrifice, he simply didn't wait.

And when the giant Goliath was taunting Israel's men,
Saul didn't have the courage to lead out even then.

When Samuel had passed away, and Saul again felt fear,
He even went and asked a witch to give him guidance clear.

David Grieves
April 11, 2 Samuel 1–2

Saul and his son Jonathan
Lie slain up on a hill.
The pride of all Israel,
Both silent now and still.

Saul was God's anointed
And David's grief was deep.
When he received the awful news,
He turned away to weep.

David wept for Jonathan,
Their love had been so pure.
And David knew a love that strong
Would help him to endure.

Joab and Abner
April 12, 2 Samuel 3–5

Saul's right hand man was Abner,
And after the death of Saul,
Abner went over to David
To help make him king over all.

Meanwhile, the main man for David
Was Joab, a cruel man at best.
When he heard David met with Abner,
He quickly set out on a quest.

Through lies and intrigue, Joab lured him
To return to Hebron that day.
Then he took him and viciously stabbed him,
And Abner died right away.

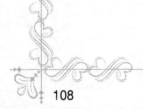

Hard Not to Question
April 13, 2 Samuel 6–9

The Ark of the Covenant was holy,
And it was specially made
With rings on each of its corners
Where carrying rods were laid.

But as David led the procession
To Jerusalem that day,
The ark rested on an ox cart
To bring it on its way.

At one point the oxen stumbled,
And Uzzah reached out his hand.
Then the Lord struck him down in anger,
And that's hard to understand.

For Uzzah just wanted to catch it.
He meant no disrespect.
But we learn from this, strict obedience
Is what our God expects.

Deeper and Deeper Into Sin

April 14, 2 Samuel 10–12

Springtime was the time of year kings led their men to war.
But David stayed behind one year and sent his men afar.

He walked upon his roof one day, and as he looked about,
There he saw Bathsheba and he quickly sought her out.

He was already married, and she was married too.
But lust became the culprit in what they chose to do.

One thing led to another until, sadly, he could see
He had planned the death of someone
who was loyal as could be.

Deeper and deeper into sin, David slipped and fell;
Setting a poor example that his sons learned much too well.

Incest in the Palace
April 15, 2 Samuel 13–14

Some folks think that money
Will bring them happiness.
Others think that power
Can cover any mess.

But listen to the story
Of a prince of Israel.
He lusted for his sister,
And the story won't end well.

First, he raped young Tamar
And then he cast her out.
Which caused his brother, Absalom,
To hate him without doubt.

Absalom killed Amnon
And then he ran away,
And neither wealth nor power could ease
The flood of pain that day.

Sins of the Father
April 16, 2 Samuel 15–16

As good a man as David was, he sometimes went astray.
And people see the things we do more than the things we say.
When David and Bathsheba broke God's law of purity,
They set a bad example deep within their family.
Amnon raped his sister, so his brother took revenge.
Now Absalom was plotting, he was on a power binge.
He sought to take the kingdom out of his father's hands
And take the role of leadership all throughout the land.
A father and his son at odds; how sad for both of them.
The flaws in David's character were playing out in him.

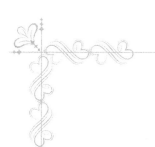

Mixed Advice
April 17, 2 Samuel 17–18

Two men were serving Absalom in giving him advice.
And so in seeking guidance, he asked each question twice.

Now Hushai was David's friend; still loyal to the king.
Ahitophel backed Absalom and sought great change to bring.

Unfortunately, Ahitophel was burdened with great pride.
And when his counsel wasn't used, he hung himself and died.

History Repeats Itself
April 18, 2 Samuel 19–20

After a war in Vietnam,
To our great nation's shame,
We treated those who fought for us
As though they were to blame.

That same mistake was made before
In Israel's history.
When David's men killed Absalom
To keep King David free.

David's men were loyal,
But David was a dad.
His heart was torn asunder.
He felt so very sad.

Joab went to David,
Reminding him these men
Had offered up their very lives
To keep him safe within.

America should listen
And learn a thing or two.
When folks lay down their lives in war,
They're heroes through and through.

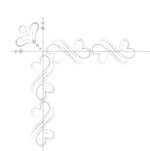

David's Poetry
April 19, 2 Samuel 21–22

We know that David loved to write when just a shepherd boy.
And as we read his poetry, we can feel his love and joy.

But David's words kept coming when he was old and gray.
He spoke of all God's blessings that guarded him each day.

He used terms drawn from nature, like fire and wind and rain.
The shepherd boy within his heart was speaking once again.

About Sacrifices
April 20, 2 Samuel 23–24

David was a shepherd,
A soldier and a king.
And he wisely turned to God
In almost everything.
So when temptation snagged him
And caught him in sin's snare,
He quickly fell upon his face
In deep and humble prayer.

When David went to Araunah
To buy his threshing floor,
Araunah offered oxen
And the wood and so much more.
But David wouldn't take it,
He completely understood;
A sacrifice that costs you nothing
Isn't any good.

David's Sons
April 21, 1 Kings 1–2

David's first son, Amnon, was a weak and sinful man.
He raped his own young sister and died by his brother's hand.

His second son, young Daniel, we don't know much about.
So by this time in David's life, the boy was dead no doubt.

Absalom was number three. We think of him and groan.
He killed his brother Amnon and then tried to take the throne.

Now David had grown older and his death was near at hand.
His promise to Bathsheba was her son would rule the land.

But Adonijah—number four—had made plans of his own.
Those plans included being king and sitting on the throne.

One Wish

April 22, 1 Kings 3–4

What if God should offer
To grant one wish for you?
Just think about it—any wish—
What would you have Him do?

Well, Solomon was granted
That opportunity.
And his request was simple:
"Grant wisdom unto me."

God was pleased with Solomon
And granted his request.
But then God added wealth and fame
And strength to meet each test.

Be careful what you ask for
When praying to the Lord.
But if your heart is true and pure,
You may reap great reward.

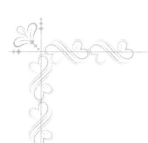

Building Projects
April 23, 1 Kings 5–7

The foundation of the temple finally was laid
When Solomon had reigned four years and preparations made.

There was cedar sent from Lebanon by Hiram, king of Tyre.
And boards of pine to make the floor
and workers he could hire.

Seven years and six months more, it took them to complete.
And then they built his palace, and that too was quite a feat.

Next came all the furnishings, each made by David's plan.
Every worker and each artist was a dedicated man.

Dedication of the Temple
April 24, 1 Kings 8

Though he oversaw the building of a temple of renown,
Even Solomon knew that God could not,
by walls of stone, be bound.
But he stood before the altar with his hands held open wide
And he praised the God of heaven
with the people close beside.

Then he turned and blessed the people
and reminded them that they
Must be loyal, faithful servants as they went about each day.
Sacrifices then were offered, by the
thousands they were brought.
Such a time of dedication as God's favor each one sought.

A Visit from a Queen

April 25, 1 Kings 9–11

When it comes to wealth and riches,
Just picture, if you can,
Twenty-five tons of gold each year
Given to one man.

The Queen of Sheba visited
To see if it was true
That Solomon was really wise
In all he sought to do.

She brought him gifts of precious stones
And gold and spices too.
She tested him with questions
Just to see what he would do.

Amazed at all his wisdom,
His palace, and his throne,
She praised the God of heaven
Then she left to go back home.

A Kingdom Divided
April 26, 1 Kings 12–13

In one little verse of Scripture, we learn of Solomon's sin:
"He loved many foreign women" and
each brought her own god in.

So God announced his judgment, and
when Solomon passed away,
The kingdom became divided and sadly remained that way.

In the South was Rehoboam; Judah's king and Solomon's seed.
But the other ten tribes of Israel followed Jeroboam's lead.

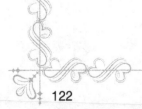

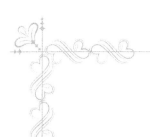

Wicked Kings
April 27, 1 Kings 14–15

Jeroboam—Israel's king—was a wicked, foolish man.
He made a golden calf to put in each end of the land.
God struck his son with illness, and Jeroboam sent
His wife to ask the prophet exactly what this meant.

Ahijah was the prophet, and as soon as she appeared,
He warned her that her son would die just as she had feared.
Abijah, Jeroboam's son, died just as God had said.
And then a son named Nadab ruled just like his dad had led.

Elijah
April 28, 1 Kings 16–18

Elijah was a prophet;
A man both brave and bold.
And every generation
Should hear his stories told.

God sent him into hiding
In a time of Israel's drought.
And ravens brought him bread and meat.
He never did without.

Then in Zarephath one day,
A widow's faith was used.
God kept her jar of flour full
And oil within her cruse.

One day upon a mountain top,
God burned the wet, wet wood.
And licked the water from the dust
Where once the altar stood.

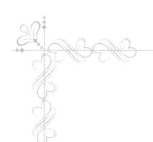

Downhearted Elijah
April 29, 1 Kings 19–20

After his great victory against the men of Baal,
Elijah was exhausted and his strength began to fail.

So when his life was threatened by the wicked Jezebel,
He fled into the desert and hid himself quite well.

Then God sent him an angel, who fed him fresh baked bread.
But Elijah was downhearted and wished that he was dead.

God sent a great and powerful wind
and then an earthquake too.
Then finally He sent a fire; a show of strength, it's true.

At last God spoke so gently that Elijah leaned His way.
**And God gave him marching orders
to return to work that day.**

A Stolen Vineyard

April 30, 1 Kings 21–22

Some folks think they have the right
To anything they see.
Even if that thing they want
Belongs to you or me.

That's how it was with Ahab,
That very wicked man.
He wanted Naboth's vineyard,
A nearby piece of land.

When Naboth wouldn't sell to him,
The king went home to pout.
But Jezebel, his wicked queen,
Stepped in to work things out.

Soon secret plans were given
Which ended Naboth's life.
And Ahab got his vineyard.
That was stolen by his wife.

A Vision of Blood
May 1, 2 Kings 1–3

Three kings had come together, their forces joined as one.
Against the king of Moab, for sins that he had done.
For seven days, they traveled to reach the chosen spot,
And when they got there, men and beasts
were thirsty, tired, and hot.
There was no water for them—the land was dry as dust.
But someone called Elisha, a man they all could trust.
"Make this valley full of ditches" was Elisha's clear command.
Not only will your thirst be quenched—
you'll soon possess the land.
God sent the water flowing, clear and clean—no sand or mud.
But in the early morning sun, the water looked like blood.
The men of Moab saw it, and thought their enemies
Had fought and killed each other off,
and they were filled with glee.
But when they came to rob them and gloat o'er all the dead,
The men of Israel rose up and fought them till they fled.

Miracles through Elisha
May 2, 2 Kings 4–5

In these two little chapters,
We see God's loving care
Working through Elisha
As he traveled here and there.

First, there was a widow
With two small boys to raise.
God caused her jar of oil to flow
To last throughout her days.

Elisha went to Shunem
And met a lady there.
She had no child until he turned
To God in earnest prayer.

We all know that our Savior
Fed crowds with fish and bread.
Elisha fed one hundred men
With twenty loaves of bread.

Nothing Too Small
May 3, 2 Kings 6–8

So many times we worry and fret when things are small.
We think we shouldn't trouble God with such a thing at all.

But while some men were working to build a brand-new place,
An ax head fell in water there and sank without a trace.

The man cried to Elisha, "The ax head wasn't mine."
I borrowed it and now it's gone, and iron is hard to find.

Elisha cut a stick and threw it where the ax head fell.
The ax head floated to the top and everything was well.

So never, ever worry. Just come to God in prayer.
If something brings concern to you, just know God also cares.

Justice for Naboth
May 4, 2 Kings 9–10

Jehu was anointed
Israel's new king.
And he was given orders;
Naboth's justice he must bring.

Destroy the house of Ahab
And Jezebel, his queen,
For all the blood that they have shed.
They're wicked and they're mean.

So Jehu went to Jezreel.
He killed Joram, Ahab's son,
And there stood wicked Jezebel,
Watching what was done.

Her eunuchs stood behind her,
And to make the job complete,
They threw her down and she was killed
Beneath the horse's feet.

Difficult Reading
May 5, 2 Kings 11–13

One problem that I seem to have when studying God's Word
Is all the funny sounding names I have never heard.
There's Rehoboam and Jeroboam, and
though that sounds like twins,
They actually were enemies and each fought hard to win.

There's Joash and Jehoash and Jehoahaz as well;
Ahaziah and Amaziah, each with a tale to tell.
And then there's Athaliah and how she took the throne.
She had her own dear grandsons slain—
her heart was cold as stone.

Jeroboam's Legacy
May 6, 2 Kings 14–15

As we read these books of history, some things are clear to see;
Like just how strong the influence of leadership can be.

Just look at Jeroboam—corrupt throughout his reign,
And wicked kings from that time on
were judged with great disdain.

Each time their story's written, we hear the writers say:
"From the sins of Jeroboam, he did not turn away."

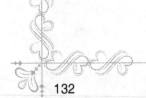

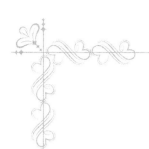

The Altar of Ahaz

May 7, 2 Kings 16–17

Ahaz, king of Judah, was as wicked as could be.
He built a pagan altar and removed the bronze sea.
He copied pagan customs—every thought and each desire.
He even sacrificed his son—an offering by fire.

A nation once so blessed by God, the apple of His eye,
Was now as wicked as the ones that God said had to die.
They worshipped many idols and set up sacred stones.
They turned away from God's command
to worship Him alone.

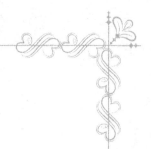

Hezekiah
May 8, 2 Kings 18–20

Hezekiah's story is quite interesting to read.
It gives us the encouragement that we so often need.

Hezekiah was a king whose faith was strong and true.
And God responded to that faith blessing all he tried to do.

He never sought for help in war from pagan kings nearby.
And when his health began to fail, God did not let him die.

But when his wars had ended and his
health returned once more,
Pride slipped in to trip him up—sin's always at the door.

So when you feel discouraged over foolish things you do,
Remember, mighty men of God had times of weakness too.

Good King Josiah
May 9, 2 Kings 21–23

Josiah was eight when he became king,
And he reigned for thirty-one years.
He did what was right in the eyes of the Lord
And eased the people's fears.

He ordered repair on the temple,
And as the work was done,
Hilkiah, the priest, found the book of the law
And went to the king on the run.

Josiah listened intently,
Then tore his robes in grief.
He understood completely
His people's lack of belief.

Josiah started a cleansing
By faithfully taking a stand.
He destroyed the idols and pagan priests
All throughout the land.

Josiah was killed in battle
As he fought against Neco, a king.
But the good that he did in the way that he led
Was truly a beautiful thing.

Jerusalem Falls
May 10, 2 Kings 24–25

Oh, how sad a story that a city so blessed by God
Could have fallen so far out of favor that
He used Babylon as His rod.

The city wall was broken—the treasures all carried away.
The people went into exile. What a sad and tragic day.

These things all happened to Judah
according to God's command;
To remove from before His presence,
the evil throughout the land.

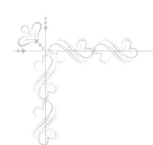

Genealogies
May 11, 1 Chronicles 1–2

If you like genealogies,
This book will pass the test.
You'll learn of sons and daughters
From the worst up to the best.

The many names here written
To us sound very strange.
And yet if they were here today,
They wouldn't want to change.

So don't be too discouraged;
Keep digging and you'll find
Some interesting connections
Within the family lines.

Jabez

May 12, 1 Chronicles 3–5

Why would a mother give her child
A sad and painful name?
A name that says to others,
"This child has brought me shame."

Yet that's what Jabez's mother did
In calling him her "pain."
Reminding him of how she felt
Time and time again.

But Jabez took his pain to God
And asked that he be blest.
Then Scripture says God heard his prayer
And granted his request.

Beriah

May 13, 1 Chronicles 6–7

Genealogies continue in our Scripture for today
And the names are very difficult and hard for us to say.

Once again we have a parent, whose poor character we find
In giving to his son a name both thoughtless and unkind.

He named his son Beriah—it's in verse twenty-three.
The name means there's "misfortune" within the family.

How can a loving parent cause such pain and strife
In giving such an awful name that one must wear for life?

Keep Reading
May 14, 1 Chronicles 8–10

Are you still with me as we read
Or have you walked away
As we go through these lists of names
That we can't even say?

We must remember that these folks
Who lived so long ago
Did not have written proof of birth
That they could quickly show.

It's hard for me to even read,
It certainly isn't fun.
And yet they memorized these lists
And passed them to their sons.

So though we may not understand
Why God has placed them there,
If we are faithful to the task,
It shows God that we care.

Super Heroes
May 15, 1 Chronicles 11–13

When we read the story of David's mighty men,
They seem like super heroes who would always fight and win.

We read of men like Abishai, who won a victory.
He killed three hundred men alone and thus made history.

Benaiah was another, who came to David's side.
He killed a tall Egyptian—by the man's own spear he died.

There were many others whose names we can't recall.
But here's the secret to their strength:
the Lord was with them all.

The Ark Comes Home

May 16, 1 Chronicles 14–16

When David first attempted
To move the ark of God,
A man named Uzzah lost his life
As by its side he trod.

The reason he was stricken
Is hard to understand.
But he was not to touch it,
Yet he reached out with his hand.

So David felt great anger
And the fear he felt was large.
But finally he tried again,
With Levites now in charge.

They offered sacrifices;
And David wrote a psalm.
Then for a while, folks went back home
And everything was calm.

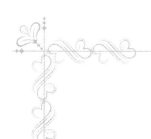

God's Promises
May 17, 1 Chronicles 17–20

David spoke to Nathan, a prophet and a friend,
And told of his desire to build a house to place the ark within.

But God said no to David and then God made a vow
That David's son would build it and
God would show him how.

God made another promise, a son of David's own
Would follow him to rule the land and sit upon his throne.

Wars broke out all around him and his men were quickly sent.
Then "The Lord gave David victory everywhere he went."

God's Word is full of promises He made to you and me.
If we are faithful to His will, those victories we'll see.

A Place for the Temple
May 18, 1 Chronicles 21–23

David took a census, and though that wasn't wrong,
It angered God that David thought his army kept him strong.

So God sent forth an angel and a plague on Israel.
King David watched as seventy thousand men of Israel fell.

David saw the angel and fell upon his face
To plead with God for mercy for healing and for grace.

Then David went to Araunah and bought his threshing floor
To build an altar to the Lord where the angel stood before.

After all was said and done, David told his men
The house of God will be built here.
Then he went home again.

Hidden Stories

May 19, 1 Chronicles 24–26

As we look through the Scripture in our reading for today,
We find long lists of jobs and names—
quite boring I would say.

We look at priests and singers; at gatekeepers as well.
Musicians and their instruments, but what does all that tell?

It tells us that the temple was organized and run,
So working all together, each job was quickly done.

But hidden in the endless lists, God drops a little clue
Of giving Heman fourteen sons and
three young daughters too.

How many other stories are buried in God's Word?
Unless we pay attention, their stories go unheard.

Preparations for the Temple
May 20, 1 Chronicles 27–29

The Lord had said to David, I know what's in your heart.
But you can't build the temple. That's not to be your part.

Solomon your son will take your place as king one day.
He will build the temple, but you can prepare the way.

So David gave his son the plans which God had given him.
He gathered gold and silver and he
weighed and measured them.

The people soon joined David to worship God above.
Bronze and iron and precious stones were given with pure love.

The people celebrated with sacrifice and prayer.
Their praises rose to God above—their laughter filled the air.

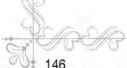

Let the Building Begin

May 21, 2 Chronicles 1–3

Solomon gave orders that the building must begin
On a temple for Almighty God, so craftsmen were called in.
Solomon sent a message to Hiram, king of Tyre,
To send him wood from Lebanon and workers he could hire.

Next, he took a census of the aliens in his land,
And then he put them all to work with foremen in command.
At last the work got started. The temple soon would stand
Where once the threshing floor had
been, but now was David's land.

Solomon's Prayer
May 22, 2 Chronicles 4–6

He knelt before the people with his hands held up on high,
As he prayed that God would listen and heed his fervent cry.

He prayed that when his people had done each other wrong
That God would act in judgment to keep the nation strong.

He prayed that when the heavens held back the precious rain,
That when the people prayed to Him,
He'd answer them again.

No matter what the reason for the troubles they went through,
He asked God to forgive them if their
hearts were pure and true.

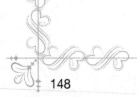

Celebration

May 23, 2 Chronicles 7–9

Once the temple had been finished
And Solomon had prayed,
The glory of the Lord came down
To bless all they had made.

The sacrifices were consumed
When fire fell from above
And people worshiped and gave thanks
For all His wondrous love.

The priests took their positions.
The Levites did the same.
All David's plans were followed
As folks praised God's holy name.

Their hearts were overflowing
For the good things God had done,
For the temple and for David
And for Solomon, his son.

Solomon's Son, Rehoboam

May 24, 2 Chronicles 10–13

What started out quite wonderful too quickly fell apart.
When Rehoboam took the throne, he didn't act real smart.

He asked advice from older men who served his father well.
But when he just ignored their words,
his kingdom quickly fell.

The northern tribes of Israel, ten of them in all,
Rebelled against the king that day and thus began their fall.

Now ruled by Jeroboam, their downfall you can trace.
The northern tribes cast out God's priests
and idols took their place.

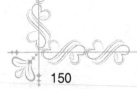

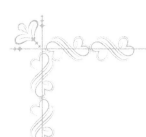

A Good King Stumbles

May 25, 2 Chronicles 14–17

Asa, king of Judah, did what was good and right.
He tore down incense altars and equipped his men to fight.

When Zerah came against him with an army that was vast,
Asa called Almighty God to hold the nation fast.

God struck down the Cushites in spite of their great size.
And Asa and his people took great plunder as their prize.

Asa then was given several years of peace and rest
Until a king of Israel came to put him to a test.

Instead of asking God to help as he did in times of old,
Asa hired another king with silver and with gold.

God sent the king a warning, but in his sin and pride,
The king would not turn back to God
and good King Asa died.

Pleasing Words
May 26, 2 Chronicles 18–20

I know you've heard it said before that some folks want to hear
Only what is pleasing to their hearts and to their ears.

Ahab was a man like that if you'll take time to read.
He only wanted prophets with whose message he agreed.

He asked the king of Judah, Jehoshaphat was his name,
To join with him and go to war for plunder and for fame.

Jehoshaphat then asked him what man of God he had.
But Ahab said, "I hate the man." His word is always bad.

Even Ahab's messenger said, "Sir, to avoid strife,
Let your words agree with theirs." It just might save your life.

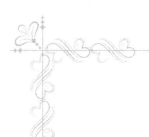

Epithet

May 27, 2 Chronicles 21–24

(Epithet: a word or phrase characterizing
a person, place, or thing.)

Most of us think of an epithet as what's
written on someone's tomb;
A short little footnote of history, not
words of doom and gloom.

So what do you think about it? What
would you want on your stone?
Something nice, I imagine, to praise
you for love you have shown.

Unfortunately, King Jehoram, was just
forty years old when he died.
And Scripture records no suggestion
that anyone grieved or cried.

In fact the epithet written was the saddest epithet yet.
It simply says, "He passed away." Then
adds, "To no one's regret."

King Uzziah
May 28, 2 Chronicles 25–27

The story of Uzziah starts out with great success.
Unfortunately, his later years were simply one big mess.

As we read these old stories, what we must always do
Is seek to find the lessons they have for me and you.

Tucked deep within his story, one simple little verse
Gives insight into where he failed and went from bad to worse

Don't miss this simple message; it's put there to impress.
"As long as Uzziah sought the Lord,
God gave him great success."

Unfortunately, over and over, we find pride creeping in.
And as we forget God's blessings, we sink ever deeper in sin.

Fathers and Sons

May 29, 2 Chronicles 28–30

Jotham was a godly king who ruled for sixteen years.
But the son who ruled right after him
would bring a man to tears.

Ahaz was the new king and Scripture tells us he,
"Did not do right in God's eyes." He was wicked as could be.

He had his men make idols and then he worshiped Baal.
He even sacrificed his sons. It is a tragic tale.

His story is a sad one, but when he passed away,
Hezekiah took the throne and sought God every day.

Manasseh
May 30, 2 Chronicles 31–33

Manasseh was just twelve years old
When he came to the throne.
But he was evil from the start
As history has shown.
He rebuilt the high places
His father had torn down,
And then built altars to the Baals
And let witchcraft abound.
Then one day, in a battle
Which Assyria had won,
Manasseh, bound in shackles,
Was sent to Babylon.
At last he sought the favor
Of Almighty God above.
And in His mercy, God reached down
And touched him with His love.
God brought him back to Judah.
He got a brand-new start.
This time Manasseh served the Lord
Renewed in mind and heart.

The Fall of Jerusalem
May 31, 2 Chronicles 34–36

Josiah was the last good king
To rule on Judah's throne.
He brought about great changes
To ensure God's will was known.

But when he died, Jehoahaz,
Was next to take that role.
He only ruled for three short months.
Then Egypt took control.

Eliakim was chosen
And they quickly changed his name.
He then was called Jehoiakim,
And evil was his game.

Next Babylon attacked him
And carried him away,
And left behind Jehoiachin—
T'was not a better day.

Zedekiah was the last,
And he just proved it true
That when you do not follow God
He soon will punish you.

God sent the king of Babylon,
Who killed both young and old,
And stripped the temple and the king
Of their treasures of pure gold.

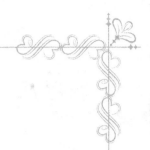

Cyrus, King of Persia
June 1, Ezra 1–2

Within the book of Ezra, it's interesting to see
How God works out His purposes and fulfills prophecies.

Jeremiah prophesied the Jews' captivity
Would last for seventy long years before they were set free.

Babylon had fallen. Cyrus now was in command.
He gave the Jews their freedom to rebuild the Holy Land.

The thing that makes this awesome,
Isaiah called him by his name,
One hundred fifty years before his birth—much less his fame.

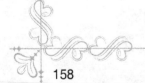

Joy and Weeping
June 2, Ezra 3–5

Coming back together,
The Israelites returned
To build again their temple
Which had been destroyed and burned.

In the seventh month they gathered,
And the first thing that they did
Was rebuild the altar of the Lord
Just as the Lord had bid.

They brought their sacrifices
And offerings galore,
And then they celebrated
All the sacred feasts and more.

The foundation of the Temple
Of the Lord was finally laid.
Then many shouted out in joy,
While others wept and prayed.

Some of them remembered
The glory days of old
When the temple built by Solomon
Was a treasure to behold.

A Plan Backfires
June 3, Ezra 6–7

Now listen little children and follow if you can,
The way that God used pagan kings to carry out His plans.

Some evil men of Persia tried to stop the building plans,
So they sent a letter to the king to ask him for a ban.

But when King Darius had a search of royal archives made,
He found King Cyrus had approved and plans already laid.

So Darius sent an order that the building should proceed.
And all the costs be taken from the royal treasury.

He warned the troublemakers they were not to interfere,
And asked the Jews to pray for him and all those he held dear.

Ezra's Prayer
June 4, Ezra 8–9

Ezra was a godly man, as faithful as could be.
He studied and applied God's Word and taught it faithfully.
When Ezra led a group of folks back home from Babylon,
The king gave his permission and supplies to carry on.
When they got to Jerusalem, they learned to their dismay,
The Jews had intermarried. So Ezra knelt to pray.
And how he prayed that so stood out
and seemed unique to me,
Was he didn't say, "Lord *they* have sinned."
Instead, he prayed, "Lord, *we*."
I wonder just how often we willingly would share
The guilt of friends or loved ones when
we lift them up in prayer.

Repentance for Intermarriage
June 5, Ezra 10

God had told His people, "Do not marry foreign wives.
They'll turn your hearts away from me
and thus destroy your lives."

But many of the exiles had disobeyed this Word.
Even priests and Levites disregarded what they heard.

So Ezra wept before God with deeply troubled heart.
How could he turn them back to God?
Where would he even start?

At last the people understood from Ezra's bitter tears
God's great anger at their sin and they were filled with fear.

The people made a covenant to send their wives away
And even children that they had were not allowed to stay.

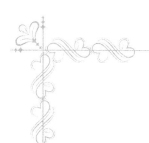

Nehemiah
June 6, Nehemiah 1–3

Nehemiah was a man of great integrity,
And though he served a pagan king, he did so faithfully.

He was the king's cupbearer—a most important task.
But one day, Nehemiah's grief was more than he could mask.

"You're troubled Nehemiah. Why so downcast and sad?"
And Nehemiah thanked his God the king did not get mad.

Nehemiah told him the burdens on his heart.
The king gave him the time to go and pledged to do his part.

And so the king wrote letters to help him on his way,
And Nehemiah started for Jerusalem that day.

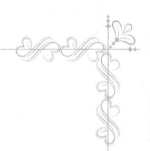

Opposition
June 7, Nehemiah 4–6

As people in Jerusalem began to build the wall,
Their enemies from all around tried hard to make it fall.

So Nehemiah had his men take swords and spears for all.
While one hand held a weapon, the other built the wall.

Another point of conflict which Nehemiah saw
Was brother charging brother, interest far above the law.

So first of all, he prayed again and asked the Lord to guide.
And then he faced the guilty ones with sin they couldn't hide.

God gave to Nehemiah, success in all his ways.
And Jerusalem's wall was finished in just fifty-two brief days.

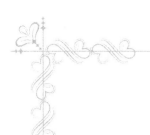

Two Good Men
June 8, Nehemiah 7–8

After the wall had been rebuilt and the gates were set in place,
Nehemiah assembled the folks to gather face to face.

He wanted them to register so everyone could see
Who could prove their lineage by their family history.

Then Nehemiah called for Ezra the priest
And all those who could understand from greatest to the least.

Once the people gathered as one within the square,
Ezra read the Book of the Law to all who gathered there.

After they had listened, each hurried on his way
To gather branches to make booths to live in seven days.

Review and Renew
June 9, Nehemiah 9–10

As all the people gathered wearing sackcloth in their shame,
They fasted and confessed their sin and
praised God's holy name.
The Book of the Law was opened and their history reviewed.
They listened very carefully and stood with hearts renewed.
You and I have Scripture, which we can read each day.
And in reading, we remember all God's great loving ways.
What about your history? Look back in quick review.
Then ask yourself this question: has God been good to you?
If God has truly blessed you and walked close by your side,
Have you in turn been faithful? Do you in His will abide?

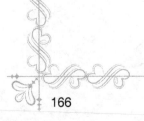

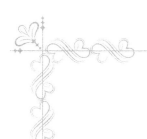

Dedicating the Wall
June 10, Nehemiah 11–12

Nehemiah asked the folks, one of every ten,
To move into Jerusalem and build their homes within.

There were priests and there were Levites.
Gatekeepers too were there;
To serve in temple services to lead in praise and prayer.

And then they came together to dedicate the wall
Which stood there fully finished, looking powerful and tall.

Their singing and their praises could be heard from far away;
As these recommitted people began to sing and pray.

Nehemiah's Prayer

June 11, Nehemiah 13

Nehemiah's faithfulness had helped rebuild the wall
That reached around Jerusalem and now stood strong and tall.
He also reinstated the law they all knew well
To keep the Sabbath holy—none could
buy and none could sell.

He called to mind King Solomon, the greatest king of all,
Reminding men how foreign wives had led the king to fall.
When all his work was finished, he turned to God in prayer
To ask that God remember all his faithful work and care.

King Xerxes
June 12, Esther 1–3

Long ago in the land of Persia,
The king made a strange request.
He called for his wife, Queen Vashti,
To come stand before his guests.

The queen knew he was drinking,
So she refused to obey.
Then the king called for his counselors
To hear what they had to say.

The fact that the queen disregarded
Her husband's direct command
Was considered an act of rebellion
And quickly spread through the land.

So the queen was sent into exile
And where her story ends,
We learn of a young girl named Esther
And how her story begins.

Haman

June 13, Esther 4–7

Haman was an evil man
Who hated every Jew.
His hatred colored every thought
And all he tried to do.

He thought he had the answer
To wipe out the Jewish race.
He didn't know Queen Esther
Would expose him face to face.

He let his pride deceive him
In what he tried to do.
For Haman didn't realize
Queen Esther was a Jew.

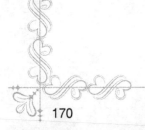

Purim

June 14, Esther 8–10

The wicked plot of Haman
To wipe out all the Jews
Backfired when Queen Esther
Told the king the news.

Her uncle, Mordecai,
Stood before the king.
He wrote new orders for the Jews
And sealed them with his ring.

The Persians stood and trembled
To see what God had done,
And no one tried to harm a Jew,
Not a single one.

A time of celebration
Was very quickly set.
The Feast of Purim, it was called.
They celebrate it yet.

Job's Friends
June 15, Job 1–5

Job was deep in sorrow; his world was upside down.
He'd lost his home and family, when
three friends came around.

Job sat among the ashes, as sick as man can be.
His friends sat down beside him in grief and misery.

For seven days they sat there, not uttering a word.
But when they finally spoke to Job, he
flinched at what he heard.

The first to speak was Eliphaz who really thought he knew
The source of all Job's problems and
the things that Job should do.

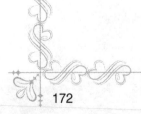

Bildad

June 16, Job 6–8

Job answered his friend Eliphaz that he could be assured
Sin was not the reason for the grief that he endured.

Job spoke of what a heavy weight his pain had brought to bear.
And how he wished Almighty God would
crush him then and there.

He criticized his friend's cold words which added to his pain;
Words which charged him with some sin that he denied again.

The second friend was Bildad, and his words were not kind.
He warned that Job should search his
heart to see what he could find.

Bildad was another who thought he knew for sure
That suffering could not occur to one whose heart was pure.

Zophar
June 17, Job 9–12

Friend number three now enters the scene,
And he is completely judgmental and mean.
He's just so sure that he is right
He even considers Job's punishment light.

Job's response is equally tart
For this so-called friend who thinks he's smart.
Job acknowledged God's strength and control
But declared the innocence of his soul.

He agreed with these men that God is strong
But still denied he had done something wrong.
He compared the strength of God to man
And wondered again at God's strange plan.

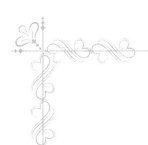

Job and Eliphaz
June 18, Job 13–16

As Job continues to try to explain
His need to understand his pain,
He speaks of how brief is the life of man
And questioned again God's final plan.

Job questions what happens after death
Once man has drawn his final breath.
But through it all, there seems to be
A thread of hope for victory.

When Eliphaz spoke once again,
His words just added to Job's pain.
A simple lesson for today:
Be careful of the things you say.

War of Words
June 19, Job 17–20

Job describes his suffering and feels his death is near.
He talks about a lack of hope to anyone who'll hear.

Then Bildad lifts his voice again, describing all who sin.
He paints an ugly picture filled with misery within.

Again Job cries for mercy against these fickle friends.
But still has hope for justice when at last this hard life ends.

Next Zophar speaks and he is sure Job's full of hidden sin.
He never really listens to the heart of his old friend.

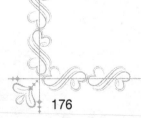

Frustration Mounts

June 20, Job 21–24

Job lashes out with bitter words
Against his faithless friends.
His anger is toward his God
And all the pain He sends.

Then Eliphaz brings charges,
And none of them is true,
Of wicked motives Job has had
In all he tried to do.

Job decides that his complaint
Is still misunderstood.
And if he could just speak to God
As man to man, he would.

So Job sets forth a litany
Of evils man has done
And spoke of how God punished them
Each and every one.

Are You Digging?
June 21, Job 25–29

It's interesting to notice as we read Job's words today
The picture that he draws for us with what he has to say.

Job spoke about the riches which God hid within the earth;
The gold and silver that men sought because of its great worth.

He spoke of all the dangers that men would gladly dare
To dig for hidden treasure as they worked in darkness there.

And then Job pointed out the truth
that men don't understand.
The greatest prize is wisdom, which God wants to give to man.

If we just took our Bibles and dug deeply, we would find
The treasures that are buried there to
help us know God's mind.

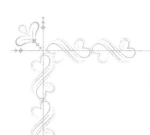

Elihu Speaks
June 22, Job 30–33

Now into the picture steps a man named Elihu.
He's listened just about as long as he is willing to.

Elihu felt great anger at the words he heard them speak.
Their arguments were foolish and their reasoning was weak.

The friends called Job a sinner whose misfortune was his own.
While Job declared his innocence of any sin he'd known.

So Elihu told each of them their arguments were wrong.
The answers they were looking for to God alone belong.

Elihu Defends God
June 23, Job 34–37

A lot of what Elihu said
Was really right on track.
He knew that God is always right
And so he answered back.

He pointed Job to heaven,
To peer into the sky,
And asked if Job could cause the clouds
To gently float on by.

He spoke of how the lightning
Is made to strike its mark
And how the very voice of God
Sends thunder through the dark.

The point that he was making
Was simple as could be.
Who was Job to question God?
But Job did not agree.

God Questions Job
June 24, Job 38–39

God had enough of listening to these men in all their pride.
They used "words without knowledge."
They were rude and they were snide.

Where were you, God asked of Job, when
I laid the earth's foundation?
Can you raise your voice to the clouds
and bring rain on the nations?

Will the wild ox consent to serve you? Will
he stay by your manger at night?
Did you clothe the horse with his flowing
mane or give to the birds their flight?

God asked Job all these questions to help him understand.
We can't understand how nature works,
how can we know God's plan?

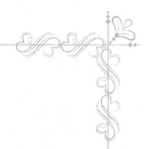

God's in Control
June 25, Job 40–42

Can you describe the behemoth a creature in this story?
Or what about leviathan in all his strength and glory?

Did you know that there are great and learned men who say
These creatures were the dinosaurs who lived back in Job's day?

Dinosaurs or crocodiles or hippopotamus,
It doesn't matter what they're called,
God made both them and us.

Job stood before Almighty God and hung his head in shame
That he had questioned God above
when times of sorrow came.

The ending of this story then brings a twist for him.
Job's so-called friends must plead with
Job to say a prayer for them.

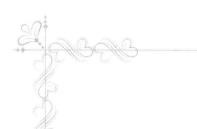

David's Psalms

June 26, Psalms 1–9

A psalm is just a song or poem to help you to express
The deepest feelings in your heart of pain or happiness.

Though David was a shepherd, a soldier, and a king,
He loved to write unto the Lord, to strum the harp, and sing.

Throughout the psalms of David, if you
read each one with prayer,
Each emotion known to man will find expression there.

There's worship and confession; there's praise and there is love.
As well as pleas that strength and help be sent from God above.

Job and David
June 27, Psalms 10–17

In Scripture, there were two great men
Who never knew each other.
And yet their hearts were so in tune
They almost seemed like brothers.

Both Job and David loved the Lord
And sought His will to know.
But both men also asked why God
Let bad men prosper so.

They recognized creation
Was His design and care.
They stood in awe of all they saw
For God is everywhere.

Another point in which these two
Would readily agree:
They both believed that after death,
The face of God they'd see.

Praise and Pleas and Prophecy
June 28, Psalms 18–22

The psalms within this section, David wrote them all.
And as you read, you quickly see God heard his every call.

Some speak of strength in battle—God-given victories.
Some speak about rejection that caused great misery.

He spoke of God's creation, of how both land and sea
Proclaim God's hand in everything and praised His artistry.

Within the twenty-second Psalm, we find such agony,
The Lord, Himself, spoke of it as He hung on Calvary's tree.

The House of the Lord
June 29, Psalms 23–30

When David speaks of "the house of the Lord,"
What do you think he is saying?
Is he speaking only of temples or churches
Where folks often go for praying?

In the twenty-third Psalm, which is known to us all,
David says he will dwell there forever.
And then in Psalm 27 he asks
That God would grant that endeavor.

It's always a blessing to gather at church,
To sing and to learn and to pray.
But I think David meant something deeper by far
As we read all that he had to say.

Since God doesn't dwell in any one place,
David may have been trying to say,
God help me and keep me so close to your side
That I live in Your *presence* each day.

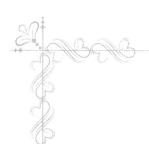

God, Our Refuge
June 30, Psalms 31–35

David saw God as a protector.
He called God his "hiding place."
He spoke of God's unfailing love for man,
And His Word which placed stars into space.

David knew armies were useless
Unless God was on their side.
And he called on the people to praise God
And plead that His love would abide.

He called God his "fortress" and "refuge."
His shelter in every storm.
He trusted God's love to protect him
And keep him from every harm.

Good Advice
July 1, Psalms 36–39

Although the words of David were written long ago,
We find them perfect for today if we would learn and grow.

He says, "Refrain from anger," and everybody knows
When anger rules, we lose control. That's just the way it goes.

He says that we should "trust" God and in His love "delight."
He tells us we should never "fret." God keeps us by His might.

And then he says, "Be still and wait." How hard that is to do.
We want to help God work things out. At least I do, don't you?

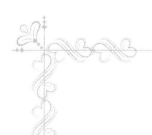

Sons of Korah
July 2, Psalms 40–45

Within the temple workers,
There was a group of men
Who served God as musicians
And they wrote psalms now and then.

They're called the Sons of Korah.
Now Korah was a man
Who led a great rebellion
Against Moses and God's plan.

Although God struck him down that day,
The rest of Korah's clan
Went on to serve God faithfully
As anybody can.

They served as choir leaders
As David had decreed.
The songs they wrote spoke of God's love
That meets our every need.

Sing Praises to God
July 3, Psalms 46–51

In one of the psalms we read today,
The sons of Korah simply say
"Sing praises to God, sing praises."

God is the King of all the earth.
We cannot measure His infinite worth.
"Sing praises to God, sing praises."

God sits upon His holy throne
And rules every nation ever known.
"Sing praises to God, sing praises."

Though many reject Him and try to deny
His very existence, one day they will cry:
"Sing praises to God, sing praises."

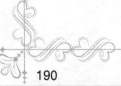

David's Faith

July 4, Psalms 52–59

In every situation, David turned to God in prayer.
When close friends turned against him,
he knew that God would care.

When armies rose against him and destruction seemed in sight,
He prayed that God would rescue him
with His great power and might.

When Saul set out to chase him in jealousy and rage,
David trusted in the Lord and war he would not wage.

David chose instead to sing with praises to his King,
And trust himself to God alone—whatever life might bring.

David's Rock
July 5, Psalms 60–66

A rock is something solid, dependable, and strong.
It doesn't simply roll away when stiff winds come along.

Oftentimes when David wrote a psalm of prayer and praise,
He spoke of God in terms of rock in many different ways.

He said that God alone would be his
"rock" and his "salvation."
He knew that only God could be a "fortress" for the nation.

A rock that he could lean on, a shelter and a shade.
As long as God was by his side, he knew he had it made.

A Word for the Elderly
July 6, Psalms 67–71

When you are tired and weary,
Your body growing old,
Look back on your life history
How you've seen God's grace unfold.

The psalmist calls them "marvelous deeds,"
These things which God has done.
And we can learn great lessons
From each and every one.

If we stop and remember
Each trial God brought us through,
We'll know He won't forsake us now.
We still have work to do.

We need to tell our children,
And our grandchildren too,
The wonders of this God we serve
That they might praise Him too.

Words of Asaph
July 7, Psalms 72–77

Many of the psalms that we are looking at today
Are credited to Asaph and he had much to say.

He wanted to remind folks of their special history
And how the awesome power of God split wide the mighty sea.

He spoke of God's creation, the sun and moon on high.
And how He caused the seasons to change as time went by.

He called God to take action against His enemies,
To punish evildoers—then he praised God's majesty.

A Word Study
July 8, Psalms 78–80

If you think you are pretty good,
Please take the time to read
The words used by our psalmists
To describe mankind's misdeeds.

When speaking of Almighty God,
Who sits enthroned on high,
They use words such as *holy*,
Offering mercy when we cry.

But when it comes to mankind,
Plain folks like you and me,
The words are *stubborn*, *proud*, and *rude*;
Disloyal as can be.

No wonder, as they're writing,
We find such heartfelt pleas
As "hear us, Lord," "restore us," and
"return to us, Lord, please."

Valley of Baca
July 9, Psalms 81–87

Look up *Baca* and you will see.
It can mean "weeping" or "balsam tree."
The sap of that tree is a tear-like gum,
Which is probably where the name came from.

The Valley of Baca was barren and dry,
But to visit the temple mount on high,
You had to travel this difficult route
Where struggles abounded, there's no doubt.

Applied to today, this picture shows,
The struggles through which a Christian goes.
It's never an easy road to trod
When attempting to draw ever closer to God.

Satan and Scripture

July 10, Psalms 88–91

Satan can quote Scripture
The same as you and I.
But when he does it, you can bet,
He uses it to lie.

The psalmist here has written
Within Psalm ninety-one,
Words about the angels
Protecting everyone.

When Jesus was His weakest,
For He knew what lay ahead,
Satan took the psalmist's words
And twisted what he said.

Instead of trusting God to send
Protection that we need,
He wanted Christ to test God
With a foolish, careless deed.

Songs of Praise
July 11, Psalms 92–100

These nine psalms, it's clear to see,
are songs of praise and victory.
We're told to "praise the Lord" on high
with "music" as the day goes by.

His deeds should fill our hearts with awe.
His works are just as is His law.
The Lord God reigns in "majesty"
and rules the mighty, pounding "seas."

God's works are "marvelous" to see.
The "rivers clap their hands" in glee.
He comes to "judge" yet He is fair.
His love surrounds us everywhere.

He stands by those who are His own
And rules from His exalted throne.
Let us "bow down" and "worship" Him,
And sing a song of praise, a hymn.

On the Wings of the Wind
July 12, Palms 101–105

From everlasting to everlasting, God's love remains the same.
And in His love He watches out for those who call His name.
He clothes Himself in splendor, and rules in majesty,
And when He speaks, the thunder rolls
across the mountain peaks.
He set the earth's foundation and filled its mighty seas.
He put in place the wild life and planted all the trees.
He makes the clouds His chariot and rides on wings of wind.
Let all creation sing His praise for all the gifts He sends.

His Unfailing Love
July 13, Psalms 106–107

The two psalms that we read today
Put God's great mercy on display.
They tell of His great faithfulness
In spite of all our waywardness.
When we're in trouble and cry out,
The Lord will hear our every shout.
He heals the sick, the blind, the lame,
And we should praise His holy name.
Repentance is the golden key
Which frees from sin and sets us free.

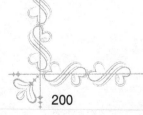

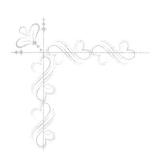

Tiny Song, Giant Truth
July 14, Psalms 108–118

Just two short verses you will find
In Psalm one seventeen.
It starts and ends with "Praise the Lord"
With few words in between.
And yet the message that it holds
Rings out both loud and clear.
Salvation is for *everyone*.
God holds *all* people dear.
So when you read your Bible,
Just open it and look,
You'll find this tiny chapter
In the middle of the Book.

God's Word
July 15, Psalm 119

Look at the psalm we have today
And the wisdom it contains.
When all else seems to fall apart,
God's love and care remains.

The psalmist asked God to teach him,
To follow every law;
To give him understanding of
Each precept that he saw.

He asked that God direct his path
That he might truly find
The way to always follow Him
With all his heart and mind.

The Word of God is powerful,
A perfect lifelong guide.
If we will only study it
And in its truth abide.

Songs of Ascent
July 16, Psalms 120–131

Jerusalem sat on a hill,
And those who journeyed there,
Sang as they "ascended"
And each song was like a prayer.

They spoke of God's great faithfulness;
His ever watchful care.
His peace and sweet security
Surrounds us everywhere.

David posed the problem,
If God weren't on our side,
The enemy would soon have won
There'd be no place to hide.

The Lord must be the builder
Or the house will never stand.
These psalms help us remember
God is sovereign over man.

God's Love Endures Forever

July 17, Psalms 132–138

God made the stars in the heavens,
The sun and the moon up above.
But the only thing lasting forever
Is God's enduring love.

God knows His chosen people.
He calls each one by name.
And even when we fail Him,
His love remains the same.

When enemies gather around us,
And it seems our end is near,
God steps in and wins the battle,
For He holds us very dear.

When sin and confusion surround us,
And we turn to God and cry,
He wipes away every teardrop.
The well of His love won't run dry.

God Our Refuge
July 18, Psalms 139–143

When David was in trouble,
He cried to God above.
"Rescue me from evil men"
By Your abiding love.

Protect my life from evil
When violent men draw near.
Remind me of Your mercy
When my heart begins to fear.

The Lord my God is sovereign.
The righteous praise His Name.
His love endures forever,
Putting evil men to shame.

Attributes of God
July 19, Psalms 144–150

Great is the Lord and worthy of praise.
He cares for His people all of their days.

Gracious is He and compassionate too.
He walks beside us in all that we do.

The Lord is good with mercy for all.
He upholds those who stumble and fall.

The Lord is righteous and always the same.
May we never stop praising His Holy Name.

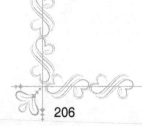

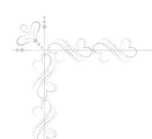

Solomon's Proverbs
July 20, Proverbs 1–3

A proverb is a saying,
Sometimes short and sweet.
That teaches us how we should act
Toward everyone we meet.

We all have heard of Solomon,
A king in days of old.
And how he asked for wisdom
Instead of lands or gold.

God gave him what he asked for,
And we can clearly see
His many, many proverbs
Share wise words with you and me.

Listen, My Son
July 21, Proverbs 4–7

The words for today are from father to son.
The earliest way that teaching was done.
The father's wisdom could be found
In these little stories handed down.
He used an ant to illustrate
That laziness won't fill our plate.
And when it comes to friends we choose,
There too are guidelines we should use.
The father then went on to say
That lust can lead your heart astray.
So listen, my son, and learn what I say
That wisdom might guide you in all your ways.

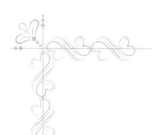

Seek Wisdom

July 22, Proverbs 8–11

Good kings reign by wisdom
And rulers make laws that are just.
Those who love wisdom are prudent.
They turn from evil and lust.

When wisdom speaks, we must listen.
She has worthy things to say.
Her instruction is better than silver,
And she's willing to guide us each day.

Wisdom is from the beginning,
From before the world began.
She stood by God's side at creation
And rejoiced when He created man.

So man would be wise to listen,
To seek her every day.
For life and favor come from the Lord
And wisdom shows us the way.

A Wise Man

July 23, Proverbs 12–15

A wise man is described for us
In many different ways.
It's said he listens to advice;
His lifestyle earns him praise.

We're told his tongue brings healing.
His words don't bite or sting.
He heeds his dad's instructions
As he seeks to learn each thing.

His teaching is a fountain,
Bringing life to all who hear.
His reverence for the Lord is shown
By service and by fear.

A wise man shuns all evil
While fools soon lose their way.
He tries to teach men knowledge
As he goes from day to day.

Gossip
July 24, Proverbs 16–19

Gossip is an evil
We are often warned about.
It never does a bit of good
Of that there is no doubt.

It separates the closest friends
And that should never be.
A friend belongs beside you
Throughout all adversity.

Gossip is an evil fruit.
Its words can seem so sweet.
The tongue has power of life and death.
Be careful what you eat.

Sharing
July 25, Proverbs 20–22

Scripture has a lot to say
About our need to share.
And only as we heed those words
Will people know we care.

We're told that if we close our ears
Against a poor man's cry,
A day will come when we have needs
And others pass us by.

But if our heart is generous
And we are quick to share,
The Lord Himself will bless us
And will meet our every care.

Then Solomon reminds us
That his words are wise and true.
As we reach out to others,
God will guide in all we do.

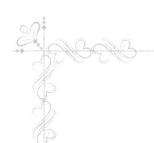

Honey

July 26, Proverbs 23–26

Honey, Scripture tells us,
Is something we should eat.
Honey from the honeycomb
Is quite a special treat.

But later comes a warning,
A message clear and bold,
Eat just enough but not too much,
Or you'll be sick, we're told.

The warning is repeated
To be sure it's understood.
Honey may be good to eat,
But too much isn't good.

Various Sayings
July 27, Proverbs 27–31

Do not boast about tomorrow;
There may be no tomorrow for you.
And do not brag about yourself.
That's for someone else to do.

Don't give yourself over to anger,
But keep yourself under control.
Don't fail to teach your son discipline,
And he'll bring delight to your soul.

Though ants are tiny creatures,
They store food for the winter ahead.
And while locusts have no leader,
They march in ranks, it is said.

When it comes time to choose a woman
To stand by your side as your wife,
Consider a woman of virtue
Who will value your love all her life.

Solomon Looks Back
July 28, Ecclesiastes 1–4

Late in life, King Solomon sat down to summarize
The many lessons he had learned and
why folks called him wise.

To read Ecclesiastes is really quite a chore.
There's sadness and depression, but look
deep—there's so much more.

Solomon recounted the many things he learned,
The things he bought or built or wrote,
and yet his heart still yearned.

There is no satisfaction that this life can provide
Unless we do it all for God and in His will abide.

Fear God
July 29, Ecclesiastes 5–8

What does it mean when we're told to fear?
Does that mean God doesn't want us near?

Does Solomon mean we should tremble and shake
In terror of making a simple mistake?

No, Solomon knew that would never do.
That is not what he's saying to me and to you.

The kind of fear he is talking about
Is an understanding of what God's about.

It's an awestruck feeling of reverence and love;
It's humbly accepting His rule from above.

It's knowing He cares for your every need.
And that, my friend, is awesome indeed.

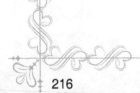

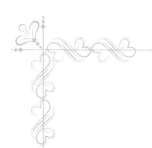

The Conclusion

July 30, Ecclesiastes 9–12

No matter how much you study,
No matter how hard you work,
You never will find true meaning
Where sin and error lurk.

Remember that life is fleeting,
And in death you soon will rest.
Your goal in life should always be
To give God your very best.

When there seems to be no justice
And life seems so unfair,
Remember that God will someday bring
True justice everywhere.

My Struggle
July 31, Song of Solomon

I always have a struggle
When I come to this small book.
Its message is so personal,
I hate to even look.

I know that true love can be found.
It's beautiful and rare.
But I think there are certain things
A person shouldn't share.

Another problem that I have,
It isn't like the king
Was so in love with this young girl
She was his everything.

With seven hundred royal wives
And concubines galore,
His words ring hollow to my ears,
She's just one of many more.

Sins like Scarlet

August 1, Isaiah 1–4

God called upon Isaiah to let His people know
They were a sinful nation whose religion was just show.

The sacrifices offered were shallow acts at best.
And when it came to serving God, they simply failed the test.

God warned their sins were scarlet—a deep, unyielding stain.
And yet if they turned back to Him they could be clean again.

The message that was given by Isaiah long ago:
If we will serve Almighty God, He'll wash us white as snow.

His Anger Is Not Turned Away

August 2, Isaiah 5–9

God was very angry
With His people long ago.
And often sent His prophets
With the words to tell them so.

Isaiah was just one of them
Whose words of warning came
To let them know their enemies
Would turn their pride to shame.

God used the foreign nations,
Bringing war and famine too,
But still His people didn't turn
As they were warned to do.

And so Isaiah told them
In words as clear as day,
Since you ignored His warnings
"His anger is not turned away."

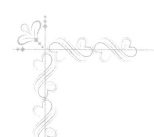

A Remnant

August 3, Isaiah 10–14

All throughout the Bible
Where judgment is foretold,
God promises a remnant
That will see His plan unfold.

When God brought forth His judgment
To punish Israel's sin,
He said a remnant would return
To serve Him once again.

A remnant is a portion
That's usually rather small;
A fraction of what came before—
Not very much at all.

But through that tiny portion,
God's plans continue on,
And mankind still has hope because
Of mercy He has shown.

Israel's Enemies
August 4, Isaiah 15–21

Isaiah's message was hard to hear.
He warned the judgment of God was near,
And His enemies had every reason to fear.

Like over-ripe figs, the armies fell.
Moab, Damascus, and Cush as well,
All named by Isaiah before they fell.

All had been thorns in Israel's side;
A sin which God would no longer abide,
And Isaiah warned there was nowhere to hide.

Death and destruction as prophesied;
A people defeated, sat down and cried.
The few who were left were terrified.

Tyre's Seventy Years
August 5, Isaiah 22–26

Nation after nation has seen God's loving hand.
Yet very few have ever come to understand His plan.

God wants to love and bless us, but in return requires
That we give Him our loyalty, forsaking life's desires.

Isaiah warned the nations from Tyre to Babylon
That when the Lord stretched out His
hand, they'd find their power gone.

But even in His judgment, God's mercy still shines through.
He set a time of seventy years for what He planned to do.

False Hope
August 6, Isaiah 27–31

Over and over in Scripture,
God's people are carefully told:
Do not look for help from Egypt.
Don't give them your silver and gold.

Why do we look for assistance
From nations who seem to be strong,
Instead of trusting Almighty God
To whom real power belongs?

Isaiah promised the people
That as soon as God heard their cry,
He would answer with rain for their gardens
And wipe every tear from their eyes.

But the people did not want to listen.
This was not what they wanted to hear.
Their trust was in empty rituals.
They did not believe judgment was near.

Hezekiah Trusts God

August 7, Isaiah 32–37

Sennachrib sent envoys to warn the Israelites.
His army was preparing to wage a mighty fight.

He said to Hezekiah, "What hope is there for you?
Your God cannot protect you, so what is there to do?"

He spoke of other nations, whose gods had let them down.
But Hezekiah listened and firmly stood his ground.

Then Hezekiah went up to the temple in alarm.
And there God reassured him He would
save him from all harm.

The angel of the Lord went out and killed so many men
That Sennachrib returned back home and never came again.

Fifteen More Years
August 8, Isaiah 38–42

God's prophet named Isaiah
Took a message to the king.
Death is coming for you,
Set in order all your things.

Hezekiah's answer was
To turn to God in prayer,
Reminding God how faithfully
He'd served with trust and care.

God heard his tearful pleading
And granted to the man
Another fifteen years of life
And victory for his land.

Then God went one step farther
To prove the words He spoke.
He turned the sun dial's shadow back
Ten steps in one quick stroke.

Why Worship Idols?

August 9, Isaiah 43–46

An idol is worthless, it's plain to see.
It cannot listen, it cannot see.
It cannot move from place to place,
So how can it offer protection or grace?

It may be silver or even gold,
But it still can't save you from your enemy's hold.
Only God is God, the great Three-in-One:
Father and Spirit and Precious Son.

So why would you ever bend your knee
To something made from a stone or a tree
Instead of the Father in Heaven above
Who gives you life and tender love?

Isaiah Continues
August 10, Isaiah 47–51

As Isaiah's words continue—words
which came from God on high.
He speaks of strength and judgment
and he gives the reasons why.

The nations were not loyal, even Israel fell away.
And each would face a Holy God and have a Judgment Day.

But every time the prophet spoke to those God called His own,
He offered reassurance that they did not stand alone.

God said, "I'm your Redeemer. I am the Lord your God."
He promised to direct their paths like a shepherd's guiding rod.

He said that His salvation, forever would remain.
And He promised the Messiah would
with love and mercy reign.

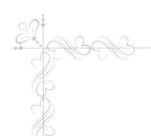

The Suffering Messiah Described
August 11, Isaiah 52–57

It's said He had no beauty or majesty to see.
He was a man of sorrows as despised as He could be.

His face was so disfigured that people were appalled;
Crushed for the iniquities committed by us all.

And though He was afflicted, He uttered not a word.
Led like a lamb to slaughter, no angry cries were heard.

It was God's will to crush Him and that His death would be
The perfect sacrifice to pay sins' debt for you and me.

Empty Fasting
August 12, Isaiah 58–63

A fast was meant to focus
Your body and your mind.
To set aside all worldly cares
And seek God's will to find.

It wasn't just avoiding
Partaking of a meal.
No, it was meant to be a time
To make your worship real.

God said on days of fasting,
If you do as you please,
Exploiting folks and quarreling,
Don't even bend your knees.

You're going through the motions.
You're putting on a show.
You may fool those around you,
But God will always know.

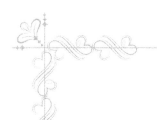

Dramatic Contrast
August 13, Isaiah 64–66

Isaiah ends his writing with
A warning to compare
The judgment that is coming
To God's blessings and His care.

He said the one God cares for
Is humble and contrite;
One who trembles at His Word
And seeks to do what's right.

But those who choose to go their way,
The arrogant and proud,
Will find themselves before Gods' throne—
Their judgment swift and loud.

Isaiah gave full warning
And ended with a plea
That those who wish to serve the Lord
Would come on bended knee.

A Faithful Prophet

August 14, Jeremiah 1–3

Jeremiah served the Lord in Judah's final days.
He warned the people daily of their selfish, wicked ways.

The symbolism that he used was really quite impressive.
His words were simple, strong, and true,
a speaker most expressive.

He classified the nation as a shameful prostitute
And warned that God would punish
her and make her destitute.

But through it all, he called to them, time and time again,
Return, you faithless people, God will then forgive your sin.

Warnings of Judgment
August 15, Jeremiah 4–6

Think about the headlines on the early morning news.
They scream of coming judgment unless
people change their views.

Flee for safety, people; raise the signal high.
Disaster and destruction loom. This is God's judgment cry.

Jeremiah warned them their punishment was near.
But people there had closed their ears
and simply wouldn't hear.

This happened in Jerusalem in days now long gone by.
But these same warnings serve today as guides for you and I.

Jeremiah Weeps

August 16, Jeremiah 7–10

Jeremiah loved the Lord,
His people, and his land.
He poured his heart out preaching,
But they would not understand.

He cried out in his agony
And told God of his grief.
He said, "I'm crushed and how I mourn."
But there was no relief.

He used the illustration
Of a fountain filled with tears.
And how he wept both day and night
Amid the people's jeers.

The land was ruined and wasted
Like a desert—dry and bare.
Because they turned from God's pure law
And served their idols there.

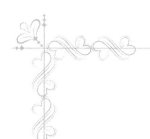

The Big Questions
August 17, Jeremiah 11–14

"Why does the way of the wicked prosper?"
"Why do the faithless live at ease?"
These are really big questions.
God, would you answer them please?

Some of the great men of history,
Men whose great faith did abound,
Have struggled with these very questions.
But very few answers were found.

Isaiah asked those questions.
And Job asked them as well.
Even Solomon inquired
To see if God would tell.

God doesn't always answer
In ways we think He should.
But we can safely trust in Him.
His ways are always good.

Four Kinds of Destroyers
August 18, Jeremiah 15–18

God spoke through Jeremiah chilling words of prophecy
Of four kinds of destroyers that would be their destiny.

The first to come would be a sword that came to them to kill.
The second one—wild dogs would
come to drag them off at will.

Birds of the air would be the next, soon
joined by mighty beasts.
They would devour and destroy and have a frightful feast.

God cursed the man who puts his trust in any other man
Instead of trusting in the Lord and His all-powerful hand.

Harsh Words of Judgment
August 19, Jeremiah 19–22

God said to Jeremiah, speak my message loud and clear.
Tell this rebellious nation that their Judgment Day is near.

I am going to bring disaster on the people of this land.
In Judah and Jerusalem, I'll ruin all their plans.

The siege will be so terrible, they'll eat each other's flesh.
And what is left, the birds will eat.
There'll be no grain to thresh.

Just like a jar that's broken and cannot be repaired.
Almighty God will smash them and not one will be spared.

Two Baskets of Figs
August 20, Jeremiah 23–25

God often taught with symbols, as we've already seen,
To help His people understand His
words and what they mean.

Therefore, to Jeremiah, God showed a vision rare
Of two large fruit-filled baskets that could not be compared.

The fruit of one was good and sweet
that folks could brag about.
The other fruit was just so bad it had to be thrown out.

God said the good fruit was a sign of
folks He would bring back.
Folks whose hearts would turn to Him
and be saved from attack.

The bad fruit was the people who had followed not His plan.
They sought instead their own wrong
ways and could no longer stand.

Jeremiah's Yoke

August 21, Jeremiah 26–28

Made of wood, a yoke would hold
Two animals as one.
That both of them together
Could get a big job done.

But God told Jeremiah,
Make a yoke for you to wear
To symbolize the bondage
Men will soon be called to bear.

Then Hananiah took the yoke
And broke it right in two;
Refusing to accept the words
Of God as being true.

So God told Jeremiah,
Go tell that foolish man,
The next yoke will be made of iron.
Break that one if you can.

I Will Be Found

August 22, Jeremiah 29–31

In writing to the exiles in the land of Babylon,
Jeremiah told his folks that they should carry on.

Build houses there to live in; plant gardens there as well.
For God sends you a promise in this
new land where you dwell.

God said if you will seek Me and pray with all your heart,
I will be found of you and that's a promise on My part.

And someday, in Jerusalem, where once you safely trod,
Again you'll be My people, and I will be your God.

And now these long years later, this promise still holds true.
Christ says if you will look for Me, I will be found by you.

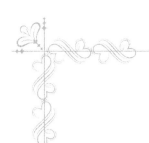

His Uncle's Field

August 23, Jeremiah 32–33

Jeremiah was confined—a prisoner of the king—
Because he spoke the truth of God, of
judgment He would bring.

But as God spoke of judgment, He also gave His word
That many would return again to rebuild homes and herds.

To illustrate His promise, God sent a special man,
Jeremiah's uncle, to sell a piece of land.

If Jeremiah bought it, then folks would clearly see
That he believed the words he preached
and all their doubts would flee.

Special Vows
August 24, Jeremiah 34–36

So many times in history, special vows were taken;
Times of dedication with certain things forsaken.

For instance, there's the Nazarite, a vow of separation
When any product of the vine was not to be partaken.
In this vow, hair could not be cut and
beards could not be shaved
And touching a dead body was not how they behaved.

And then there were the Recabites, who took a special vow
To keep a code of conduct set by those gone on by now.
Two hundred years, they followed the vow to drink no wine,
To never, ever build a house or plant a single vine.

So God, through Jeremiah, used their faithfulness to teach
A lesson on obedience in actions and in speech.

Ebed-Melech

August 25, Jeremiah 37–40

Zedekiah was a king who wasn't very brave.
When men sought Jeremiah's life, no argument he gave.

They took him to a cistern and dropped him down inside.
And though there was no water there,
the mud had never dried.

Then stepped up Ebed-Melech to stand before the king.
The treatment of God's prophet was just an awful thing.

The king gave his permission and the prophet soon was free.
Then God sent word to Ebed—you'll be glad you trusted Me.

This city now is facing disaster for its sin,
But don't you fear, I'll rescue you, and you'll be safe again.

Arrogant Stubbornness
August 26, Jeremiah 41–44

The people asked the prophet,
If you'll seek God for us,
We'll do what'ere He asks us to
And never raise a fuss.

God said to all the people,
As clearly as could be,
Do not go down to Egypt
If you would follow Me.

But did the people listen?
Did they obey His word?
No. Here's the simple answer
They gave to all they heard.

We will not listen to you!
(These people never learn.)
We'll serve the Queen of Heaven
And to her our incense burn.

God's Promise to Baruch

August 27, Jeremiah 45–48

There once was a man named Baruch
Who was known as a scribe by trade.
Scribes were experts versed in the law
And by them new copies were made.

Baruch held a special position
As both secretary and friend
To the prophet Jeremiah
Who preached of judgment on sin.

Baruch was filled with sorrow.
In pain, he could find no rest.
But Jeremiah brought him a message:
God knew he had given his best.

Although judgment truly was coming
All throughout the land,
God, Himself, would protect him,
Hidden safe in His holy hand.

God Punishes the Nations
August 28, Jeremiah 49–50

Jeremiah's message continued to explain
The nations which would suffer for causing Israel's pain.

The Ammonites and Edomites, Damascus and Kedar;
Some of them were close at hand and others very far.

Hazor and Elam, Babylon as well,
Together they surrounded the land of Israel.

Although God had allowed them, great victories to win
The time had come for all of them to suffer for their sin.

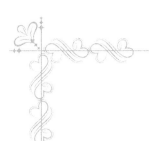

Final Vision
August 29, Jeremiah 51–52

Zedekiah wouldn't listen no matter what was said,
Though Jeremiah told him he was going to end up dead.

But sadder than the death he faced was Zedekiah's plight.
For the final things he witnessed before he lost his sight.

After he was captured, the king of Babylon
Slaughtered all his precious sons, while he was looking on.

Then he put out Zedekiah's eyes that the slaughter he had seen
Would be his final vision—a memory cruel and mean.

A Funeral Song

August 30, Lamentations 1–2

Jerusalem had fallen—
People dead or led away—
And Jeremiah wept in grief.
He'd warned them of this day.

The Book of Lamentations
Is a book of grief and pain.
It warns us of the price of sin
When we let evil reign.

Jeremiah's heart was grieved
For even children died.
The elders sat upon the ground
In sackcloth as they cried.

God punished all of Israel
In anger and great wrath.
And if you look around, you'll see
We're following in their path.

A Plea for Restoration

August 31, Lamentations 3–5

Jeremiah asked the Lord
To turn away His wrath;
To lead His children once again
Upon a pleasant path.

He asked God to return to them
The songs they once had sung;
When joy and laughter filled the streets
And bells had loudly rung.

He pleaded for the children,
Whose death was very near,
And for the mothers in whose eyes
The agony was clear.

Jeremiah had a heart
For all within his land.
And prayed for God's great mercy.
Oh, that we'd take such a stand.

Visions by the Kebar River
September 1, Ezekiel 1–4

The temple in Jerusalem for many years had been
A symbol of God's presence where He would meet with men.

But now the land of Israel in ruined shambles lay.
The people were in exile in a country far away.

So God sent them Ezekiel, whose name means "God is strong,"
To tell them God still loved them and was with them all along.

God sent Ezekiel visions and warned that he would be
Rejected by the people but still faithful he must be.

From creatures with four faces to a wheel within a wheel,
God sent him strange new visions—terrifying yet so real.

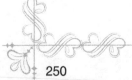

A Close Shave
September 2, Ezekiel 5–9

God said to Ezekiel, shave your beard and shave your head
For that will be a picture of the judgment that's ahead.

To shave one's beard and head was understood to be a sign.
A symbol of deep mourning—grief within the heart and mind.

Then God told Ezekiel to gather up the hair,
Divide it into three small piles as though he meant to share.

One third of it he'd burn with fire, with
the sword he'd strike one third.
And the final third he'd scatter to the
wind to spread God's Word.

Each of these strange actions would be a picture clear
Of the kinds of judgment God would send
and that day was drawing near.

A White-Washed Wall
September 3, Ezekiel 10–13

When God spoke to Ezekiel about a "flimsy wall,"
He spoke of the false prophets who were headed for a fall.

He said the many lies they told were
"washed" with coats of white
To make them look enticing so that
folks would think them right.

But trust them not, the Lord said, I'll send a cleansing rain
And hailstones that will tear them down to never stand again.

Be sure the words you follow come straight from God above.
And don't be fooled by "white-washed walls"
that lead you from God's love.

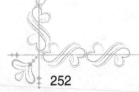

Noah, Daniel, and Job
September 4, Ezekiel 14–16

Think about Noah, Daniel, and Job,
some of Scriptures' mighty men.
Names even known by children for the way they battled sin.

Sometimes we try to follow the patterns of their lives,
Where love and prayer are central and faithful service thrives.

But God spoke through Ezekiel to warn the Israelites
That even these three special men
couldn't set their land to rights.

A scary thought, for certain, that the God of endless love
Would reach a point where judgment
must rain down from above.

That God's own special people had so much sin and pride,
Even praying men like these could not turn His wrath aside.

The Sins of the Father
September 5, Ezekiel 17–19

Stop blaming your parents for the things that you do,
For Scripture states plainly you'll answer for you.

Stop saying, "My dad didn't love me, you know.
For he never hugged me or told me so."

That's really sad, but the thing you must do
Is to make sure your son never says that of you.

You fathers stop trying to carry the blame.
Let your sons be the ones to bear their own shame.

For God, in His wisdom, has said it is true,
We will each bear the weight of the things which we do.

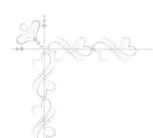

A Fork in the Road

September 6, Ezekiel 20–21

A fork in the road lay just ahead
As Babylon's king came along.
So he had to decide which road to take—
One was right and the other wrong.

He cast lots to find an answer.
He consulted his idols too.
He even examined a liver
To determine what to do.

I am so glad when faced with decisions,
I can go to the Lord in prayer.
No idols or lots to guide me
And no liver at which to stare.

Standing in the Gap
September 7, Ezekiel 22–24

God spoke to Ezekiel about the nation's sin.
He knew the time for judgment was quickly moving in.

Yet even then, it broke His heart to know what He must do.
Just read His words, you'll see His pain, and maybe feel it too.

God said, "I tried to find a man of faithful heart and mind
To stand within the gap and pray, but no one could I find."

Standing in the gap for God means spending time in prayer,
Praying for our nation and the folks for whom we care.

If God should ask of you today within the gap to stand,
Would you go willingly to pray that God might save our land?

Pagan Nations Punished

September 8, Ezekiel 25–28

Seven pagan nations
Lived around the Promised Land.
And sometimes God allowed them
To get the upper hand.

But what these nations did not see
And could not understand,
They too would soon be punished
By God's all-powerful hand.

Ammon, Moab, Edom,
Philistia, and Tyre,
These too, Sidon and Egypt,
Each one faced God's great ire.

For each of them took pleasure
When Judah suffered pain,
And none of them acknowledged God
Or sought His will to gain.

Danger of Pride
September 9, Ezekiel 29–32

"The Nile is mine," cried Egypt,
I made it just for me.
How full of pride was Egypt's heart,
Too blind to really see.
And then there was Assyria,
With strength and beauty rare,
Which like a mighty cedar tree
Gained strength beyond compare.

But God said to Ezekiel,
No more will water flow.
I'll break her limbs and dry her roots
And she will come to know:
No one is self-sufficient.
We can't live life alone.
It's only through the Grace of God
That we can carry on.

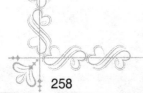

The Watchman
September 10, Ezekiel 33–36

Today we can get all the news on TV or a phone.
But in Ezekiel's day, it was by word of mouth alone.

So cities had a watchman, who stood upon the wall,
And if he spotted danger, he quickly gave a call.

If he had done his duty and still the people died,
No fault was found against him for he had really tried.

But if he saw the danger and sounded no alarm,
Then he would be found guilty for all the pain and harm.

So God said to Ezekiel, "My watchman you will be."
In all that matters spiritually, you'll warn them all for Me.

Hope In the Midst of Punishment
September 11, Ezekiel 37–39

These chapters speak of destruction
Of the death of both man and beast.
They speak of God's righteous judgment
From the greatest down to the least.

It makes for difficult reading.
We don't like the picture we see.
But the words are there for a reason.
They teach us God's great mystery.

Yes, God punishes evil,
Using war and illness and more.
But woven throughout is the promise
That God will forgive and restore.

God is always there for His children
If they only repent and obey.
He will give new life to our "dry bones"
And lead us each step of the way.

Portico?
September 12, Ezekiel 40–42

I just read these chapters and I tried to visualize
Just what they were saying, but then I realized.

I am not an architect. Their language I can't speak,
And so it's hard to clearly see the picture that I seek.

I looked in many places and felt that it was strange
How many times a simple word went through a bit of change.

Just take a look at one word: the word called *portico*.
Another version calls it *porch*, now how was I to know?

Another resource called it *arch*, another called it *jamb*.
I think I'll leave the building to the great I Am.

Holiness
September 13, Ezekiel 43–45

Scripture speaks of "holiness"—a real old fashioned word.
In fact, outside of sermons, it's rarely ever heard.

So why is it important for us to hear today;
To know if God expects us to really live that way?

The regulations given for the priests who served the Lord
Required that they do things which you
and I might find too hard.

Today, all Christians serve as priests. We come to God alone.
So holiness should be our goal as we approach His throne.

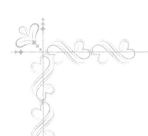

The Lord Is There

September 14, Ezekiel 46–48

Ezekiel's book is finished, and what he had to say
Reminds us that the God we serve is with us every day.

He warns us to be faithful, not to let temptation win.
And he describes the awful price that must be paid for sin.

But in the final chapters, Ezekiel ends his book
By giving us a special glimpse of how the "new world" looks.

This world will be so special—a place beyond compare—
Its name is called Yahweh-Shammah,
which means "The Lord is there."

Four Young Men
September 15, Daniel 1–3

Daniel and his three young friends were taken far away
To serve the king of Babylon and there they had to stay.
But even as they served the king in this strange pagan land,
Their faith in God was steadfast and
they followed His command.
At first, these men were offered all the finest food and wine,
But Daniel chose fresh vegetables when it was time to dine.

The king called his magicians, his astrologers and such,
To clarify a dream he had. They didn't help him much.
Then Daniel told the king his dream
and saved their lives that day.
He told him of the one true God and what He had to say.
And then you know the story of the fiery furnace planned
To punish them because they would not bow at his command.

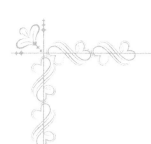

Three Stories
September 16, Daniel 4–6

Today we have three stories,
And if we read them well,
We see the sovereignty of God
And His faithfulness as well.

King Nebuchadnezzar paid a price
For letting his pride rule.
For seven years, he roamed the fields
Behaving like a fool.

Next we have the story of
The writing on the wall
And how they sent for Daniel
Who interpreted it all.

Then we have a story
Which most every child can tell.
Daniel in the lion's den
Yet how that ended well.

Highly Esteemed
September 17, Daniel 7–9

We all know the story of Daniel—
thrown into the lion's den to die.
How God sent angels from heaven and
the lions just lay down nearby.

But there's so much more to his story.
He was such a faithful man.
God sent him amazing visions of future judgments and plans.

There were visions he had while dreaming
of four beasts coming out of the sea.
And Daniel, troubled in spirit, asked
what the meaning might be.

Again, Daniel had a vision, this time of a goat and a ram.
And the angel Gabriel brought him, word from the great I Am.

Daniel was given the meaning of each
vision he saw as he dreamed,
Because, as Gabriel told him, Daniel was "highly esteemed."

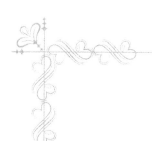

Till the End
September 18, Daniel 10–12

As Daniel grew much older,
God continued the visions He sent.
And some were so overwhelming
That Daniel's strength was spent.

At last Daniel said to the messenger,
"I heard but I don't understand."
And his answer still has a message
That should guide our thoughts and plans.

"Go your way, Daniel," the man said,
"The words are sealed till the end."
Stop worrying when things will happen
And just be ready, my friend.

The promise of rest God gave Daniel,
And resurrection someday,
Are all that we need to consider
While like Daniel, we work and pray.

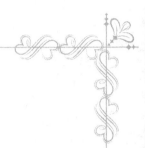

Hosea
September 19, Hosea 1–6

Hosea is a story that is difficult to read;
A story of comparisons and lessons we all need.

God said to Hosea, you must go and take a wife,
But understand that she will cause you
great heartache and strife.

The picture God was drawing for Israel to see
Was how unfaithful she had been and what the cost would be.

Though God had blessed the nation
with grain and oil and wine,
Their gold and silver treasures, they took to Baal's shrine.

Today, are we so different in the things we say and do?
God is still the great provider. It's to Him we must be true.

A Half-Baked Cake

September 20, Hosea 7–14

Would you want to eat a pancake
That was cooked on just one side?
With its top all wet and runny,
Could you eat it if you tried?

It would not be what you wanted
And would hold out no appeal.
Yet this is how Hosea
Told the people God must feel.

Such a cake is worthless.
Such a nation is as well.
And Ephraim had fallen far
As anyone could tell.

But God's heart is so tender,
His love to them He sent.
He would give them one more chance
If they would just repent.

A Call to Repentance
September 21, Joël 1–3

Joel was a prophet many years ago.
And when he preached to Judah, he let the people know
God was sending judgment, as they would surely see,
Unless they turned their hearts to God,
they never would be free.

Joel told of locusts swarming on the land;
Crops were devastated; the ground turned into sand.
There would be no grain to thresh, no fruit from any vine.
The sun and moon would darken and
the stars no longer shine.

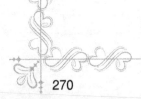

Warnings of Amos
September 22, Amos 1–5

Amos was a shepherd and a tender of fig trees.
Till God called him and told him, "A prophet you will be."
I'm sending you to Israel to warn the people there
That Judgment Day is coming. Do they really even care?

Then God gave Amos visions of the
judgments He would send,
Like locusts swarms and fire and drought and exile in the end.
He'd start with their "high places," and they would surely see
What God had meant when He had warned,
"You have not returned to Me."

Amos

September 23, Amos 6–Obadiah 1

Amos had five visions
Of judgments God would send;
Swarms of locusts, dreadful fire,
And a plumb line measuring sin.

Next, a basket filled with fruit
That looked like something great.
But it was meant to represent
The time for Israel's fate.

Finally he saw the Lord
Standing by an altar,
Warning of the wrath to come,
A time of deadly slaughter.

But Amos didn't end his words
With warnings of despair.
He offered words of peace and hope,
"Repent and you'll be spared."

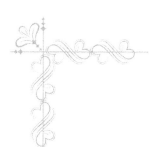

Jonah
September 24, Jonah 1–4

Jonah ran away from God and went down to the sea.
He didn't want to go and preach, so he thought he would flee.

Once on the sea, a storm arose; the sailors cried in fear.
But Jonah slept below the deck and didn't even hear.

Lots were cast and Jonah knew he was the guilty man.
"Throw me into the sea," he said, "and
you will reach dry land."

God caused a fish to swallow him, just picture such a sight.
For Jonah lived inside that fish for three days and three nights.

Walk Humbly
September 25, Micah 1–7

Micah was a prophet who lived many years ago.
And every word God gave to him, he wanted folks to know.

He spoke against the shepherds who
were sent to teach God's way.
Instead they lied and cheated and the sheep were led astray.

Micah told the people, God has shown you what is good.
It's really very simple if you do the things you should.

It isn't about sacrifice or offerings you bring.
It is the motive of your heart that counts in everything.

Act justly and love mercy; walk humbly with your God.
Then He won't have to punish you with discipline's tough rod.

Woe to Nineveh

September 26 (Part 1), Nahum 1–3

The time had come to punish. Wicked Nineveh must fall.
Though God is slow to anger, He would
now tear down her walls.

The city was full of plunder. Horses and chariots were there.
God set His face against her. It was too late now for prayer.

Habukkuk Questions God

September 26 (Part 2), Habukkuk 1–3

Habakkuk asked his questions as to why God would allow
The wicked to continue and to flourish even now.

Then he said, I'll stand my watch upon the city wall
And wait to see what He will say in answer to my call.

God answered all his questions, explaining each of them.
Habakkuk said, let all the earth be silent before Him.

God Will Punish
September 27 (Part 1), Zephaniah 1–3

Josiah was a godly king, and when God's Word was found,
He tried to get the Israelites to turn their lives around.

The prophet Zephaniah did the best that he could do
To make the people understand Josiah's words were true.

He warned them of God's judgment but offered hope as well.
If only they had listened, this would be a different tale.

Give Careful Thought
September 27 (Part 2), Haggai 1–2

Haggai, the prophet, brought word from the Lord
"Give careful thought to your ways."
Your vats are not filled with wine or with oil.
I've not blessed you in many days.

If only you did the things that you should,
But my house in ruin remains.
Give thought to your ways and I will return
The blessings of nourishing rains.

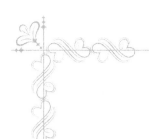

The Apple of God's Eye
September 28, Zechariah 1–7

Zechariah—man of God—a prophet and a priest.
He brought God's Word to everyone from greatest to the least.

He spoke to all the Israelites—the "apple of God's eye,"
He told them God would bring them
home for He had heard their cry.

God gave him eight clear visions of what He had in store.
Both His judgment on the wicked and His promise to restore.

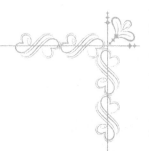

The Lord Almighty
September 29, Zechariah 8–14

The Lord sent Zechariah to speak to Israel's men
And promised them that He would bless Jerusalem again.

Zechariah wanted them to really understand,
And so he used a special phrase to introduce each plan.

This is "what the Lord Almighty" told me, I should say.
He will bless Jerusalem for you again someday.

God, the Lord Almighty, the Lord of heaven's hosts,
Our Savior and protector, in Him only can we boast.

Blemished Sacrifices
September 30, Malachi 1–4

Malachi wrote to folks much like you and me.
Messiah simply had not come, and that was plain to see.

So they had grown discouraged in keeping His commands.
Was serving God worthwhile at all? They did not understand.

The sacrifices offered were certainly not the best.
The priests gave Him no honor. They were sinful as the rest.

"I am not pleased with you," God said, and I will not accept
Such blemished sacrifices while the best ones you have kept.

God charged that they had robbed Him
and that charge holds true today.
How many tithes and offerings are folks faithful now to pay?

Matthew's Message
October 1, Matthew 1–4

When Matthew set about to write the book that we now read,
He knew his Jewish brethren had a deep and urgent need.

They looked for the Messiah who was promised long ago.
Jesus was that promised One, and Matthew told them so.

He started with the family tree to prove that only He
Was born through David's lineage and fulfilled the prophecies.

He told about the angels who announced the new-born King,
And how the Magi traveled far to see this wondrous thing.

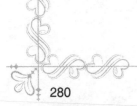

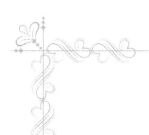

Salt of the Earth
October 2, Matthew 5–6

Jesus said that Christians are salt upon the earth,
And we must watch our attitudes if we are to have worth.

Just as salt adds flavor to everything we eat,
Our attitude can set the tone with everyone we meet.

If we are cross and cranky, our answers sharp and mean,
They certainly will not care about the Christ they haven't seen.

But if our words are gentle, as Christ would have them be,
We leave a picture of God's love for everyone to see.

Such Great Faith
October 3, Matthew 7–9

A Roman Centurion came one day,
His servant lay terribly ill.
He pleaded with Jesus to help the man,
"I know you can if you will."

Jesus offered to follow him home
And heal the man where he lay.
But the Roman said, "Just speak the word,
And his sickness will go away."

This man was a Roman soldier—
Not an Israelite for sure.
And yet he had faith in Jesus
That His word was a perfect cure.

Christ said, "In all of Israel,
Such great faith has not come My way."
Then He honored the faith of that soldier.
His servant was healed that day.

Worth More Than Sparrows

October 4, Matthew 10–11

We spend our lives staying busy,
Each day running to and fro.
And when our burdens grow heavy,
We wonder, "Does God even know?"

Well, Scripture has the answer
Written plainly, that we might see.
If God cares for tiny sparrows,
Then surely He cares for me.

He cares for each sparrow that falls to the ground,
And we are worth much more.
So much that He sent His son Jesus
To guide us to Heaven's shore.

I Desire Mercy
October 5, Matthew 12

As the Lord and His disciples
Traveled through the land,
They could not get the Pharisees
To try and understand.

The Sabbath was a gift to man
And not a limitation.
But Pharisees saw only rules
In every situation.

Jesus tried to tell them
In words both plain and clear,
Their guideline should be *mercy*
Not sacrifice and fear.

The Sabbath should be special.
With that they all agreed.
But Jesus said, in times of doubt,
Let mercy guide your deeds.

Parables

October 6, Matthew 13–14

A parable is a story—something common to compare
With something deeply spiritual you're trying hard to share.

Matthew said that Jesus taught in parables each day
In order to reach out to those who truly sought His way.

The parables were simple, using subjects they knew well,
And gave them deeper insights with each story He would tell.

He spoke of dirt to farmers, of yeast to those who bake.
He talked of fishing nets and pearls as He sat by the lake.

These simple little stories made truths ring loud and clear
And those same stories teach today if we'll take time to hear.

How Did They Know?
October 7, Matthew 15–17

Have you ever wondered, as this story you have read,
How Peter recognized these men? For
they had long been dead.

Back then there were no photographs
nor paintings folks could see.
But Peter didn't hesitate—he knew who they must be.

Moses and Elijah, both men of great renown,
And as they stood and talked with Christ,
the voice of God came down.

I wonder if this story holds a clue for you and me.
I wonder if in heaven we will know each one we see.

Little Children
October 8, Matthew 18–20

We cannot read God's Word today and not be made aware
That Jesus loves the children and provides them special care.

When followers asked Jesus who the greatest one would be,
He stood a child within their midst for all of them to see.

He spoke about a child-like faith, its sweet simplicity,
And warned that if they hurt a child,
His wrath they'd surely see.

God has a special angel assigned to every one
To guide them and to bless them for
they're precious to His Son.

Pay Your Taxes
October 9, Matthew 21–22

Paying taxes is nothing new.
Jesus had to pay them too.
But there was a line He carefully drew
About who to give our loyalty to.

As long as we live on this earth below,
There is one sure thing we need to know.
We must set an example for all to see:
That a Christian honors authority.

For God has said no one rules the land
Unless allowed by His command.
So honor God's Word and the government too,
And the Lord will bless you through and through.

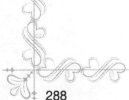

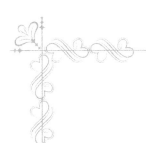

Work While You Wait
October 10, Matthew 23–24

Matthew gives us many of the lessons Jesus taught:
Words to help us understand and live life as we ought.

One important lesson that so many fail to see
Is how to wait for Jesus when He comes in majesty.

They fret about "signs of the time" and speculate on dates,
When Scripture clearly tells us to stay busy while we wait.

God didn't tell the prophets who lived so long ago.
If we stay busy serving Him, why would we need to know?

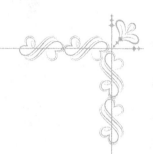

Thy Will Be Done
October 11, Matthew 25–26

The disciples asked the Lord one day
If He would teach them how to pray.
His answer was a simple one,
Your prayer should say, "Thy will be done."

Years later at Gethsemane,
Christ prayed in deepest agony.
But even then God's precious Son
Said, "Not my will, but Thine be done."

Today when we kneel down to pray,
It takes great courage when we say
In full surrender, like His Son,
God, not my will, but Thine be done.

If Christ Had Come Down

October 12, Matthew 27–28

If Christ had come down from the cross that day
In response to the taunts that were coming His way,
What would that mean for you and me?
There would be no salvation, don't you see?

The crowds saw the miracles He had done,
Yet they wouldn't believe He was God's own Son.
They wanted a warrior, a fighter, a king—
A man of war who would change everything.

If He had come down, perhaps a few
Would have believed, but then what would *we* do?
Without His death on the cross that day
Our sins could not be washed away.

I'm glad Christ made the choice He made
So the penalty for my sins could be paid.
God clearly said there was no other way,
If Christ had come down from the cross that day.

Healings
October 13, Mark 1–3

When Jesus walked the dusty roads
and went from town to town,
Folks came to Him for healings from everywhere around.

Mark tells us that the mother of Peter's wife was sickly,
But Jesus took her by the hand and
she was healed that quickly.

When a man with leprosy fell down on bended knee,
Jesus simply touched the man and he was clean and free.

One man who was paralyzed had friends who tore a hole
Right through the roof and lowered him—
to reach Christ was their goal.

When Jesus saw the faith they had, He simply spoke the Word.
The man got up and walked away and
people's hearts were stirred.

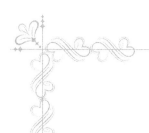

Seed

October 14, Mark 4–5

When you take a little seed and place it in the ground,
You do so hoping someday soon a green shoot will be found.

It is the earth which holds the seed
and keeps it safe from harm,
And it is God who sends the sun to keep the small seed warm.

God waters it with gentle rain; the
seed soon sprouts and grows.
And how much good can come from
that, it's only God who knows.

Jesus said the mustard seed, the smallest seed of all,
Grows into a mighty plant standing straight and tall.

And when we plant the Word of God, just like that tiny seed,
It's God who causes it to grow to meet our every need.

A Strange Request
October 15, Mark 6–7

Aladdin had a magic lamp. At least that's what we hear.
And when you rubbed it on its, side a genie would appear.

This genie granted wishes, and so a game we'd play
Was if I could have just one wish, what would I ask today?

We sometimes wished for riches or palaces so grand.
But someone's head upon a plate? That I can't understand.

Herod's young stepdaughter was given such a chance
Because she had pleased Herod with
the way that she could dance.

He offered to reward her, thinking she would ask for gold.
Instead she asked for poor John's head—a
wish both cruel and bold.

Herod gave the order and the gruesome task was done.
I think I like it better when the wishes are just fun.

A Young Boy Possessed
October 16, Mark 8–9

A father asked the disciples if they could heal his son.
The boy was possessed by a spirit and
often great harm was done.

When Jesus came down from the mountain
and saw the crowds gathered 'round,
He asked them what was happening and
was saddened by what He found.

The disciples had been unable to help the boy at all.
But the spirit was forced to leave him
as soon as he heard Jesus call.

The boy was returned to his father and
together they walked away,
While Jesus taught His disciples a lesson on how to pray.

A Barren Tree
October 17, Mark 10–11

As Jesus was leaving Bethany, He noticed a nearby fig tree.
And though its leaves were green and full,
not a single fig could He see.

Jesus pronounced His judgment: the
tree would never more bear.
Then He turned, and with His disciples,
He walked away from there.

The tree was only a picture of His sadness and dismay
At the way God's chosen people were
choosing to go their own way.

Their religious acts were showy with many an eloquent prayer,
But Jesus, who knows the hearts of men,
knew they really didn't care.

Their spiritual lives were empty. No fruit was there to see.
They didn't live up to their promise just like the barren fig tree.

The Widow's Mite
October 18, Mark 12–13

Jesus watched the people bring their offerings with delight,
And then He told a story of a widow and her "mite."

If you look up the meaning of that unfamiliar word,
You'll understand much better the lesson you just heard.

Smaller than a penny, the root word is a *flake*,
And that is such a small amount, what
difference could it make?

But Jesus told the people, although the gift seemed small,
What mattered most was not the size but that she gave her all.

Hard to Believe
October 19, Mark 14–16

Do you ever wonder if you're the only one
Who sometimes has a struggle with the story of God's Son?
Well, read the book of Mark, my friend, and you will surely see
That others also struggled so you're in good company.

When Jesus rose that morning of Resurrection Day,
He spoke to Mary Magdalene and sent her on her way.
She hurried to tell others that they didn't have to grieve,
But none of them accepted her, they just could not believe.

He later joined two others as they walked away from town,
And when they realized who He was,
they turned themselves around.
They hurried to Jerusalem and spoke to all the rest,
But they did not believe them, they were sure it was a test.

Then as they were eating, He appeared unto them all
And He rebuked their lack of faith and said they should recall
He had told them it must happen—
He would suffer and then die.
But death was not to be the end and now they could see why.

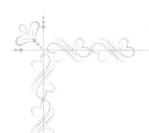

Two Mothers

October 20, Luke 1

Luke tells us the story of two women that God blessed.
Each became a mother and each withstood great tests.
Elizabeth and Mary—each one was most unique.
But each was chosen for a task, a job they did not seek.

Elizabeth was barren and was well along in years.
Back then that was disgraceful and the cause of many tears.
But God had His own purpose and in His time it was done.
Elizabeth gave birth and John the Baptist was her son.

The other one was Mary—a young girl not yet wed.
God sent the angel Gabriel to tell what lay ahead.
Mary, you've found favor and you will have a son.
He will reign forever. He is the Promised One.

Two Witnesses
October 21, Luke 2–3

Years ago, the elderly were held in high regard.
And when they shared their wisdom, folks listened really hard.
Two people at the temple, when Jesus's parents came,
To dedicate Him to the Lord, spoke out to praise His name.

The first to speak was Simeon, both righteous and devout.
He waited for the "promised one" that he had heard about.
He took the infant in his arms and looked to God above,
Content to die for he had seen the proof of God's great love.

Anna was the other—in her eighties some would say.
She never left the temple. She worshiped night and day.
When she saw the Christ child, she spoke for all to hear.
God's promise of redemption had finally appeared.

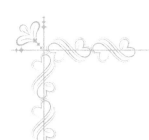

Healing Touch
October 22, Luke 4–5

Today we have such illnesses
As cancer and TB.
But in the Bible we are told
Of one called leprosy.

When someone had this illness,
They had to leave their home
And go into the countryside
Where other lepers roamed.

Their flesh would simply rot away
And fall off of the bone.
No one dared to touch them,
So they lived outcast—alone.

But Jesus met a leper
Who fell down at His feet,
And when He gently touched the man
His healing was complete.

A Simple Illustration
October 23, Luke 6–7

The little children sing a song, as cute as it can be,
Of two men who built houses with a difference you could see.

The first one built his house on sand. It quickly washed away.
The other built upon the rock. His house was built to stay.

The story comes from Scripture—a message clear and strong;
Ignoring lessons Jesus taught is dangerous and wrong.

Jesus Calms Storms

October 24, Luke 8–9

Christ and His disciples
Set out to cross the lake.
When suddenly a strong, fierce wind
Begin to toss and shake.

The Sea of Galilee was known
For storms that quickly swell,
And so their hearts were filled with fear,
They knew the dangers well.

When Jesus was awakened,
He simply spoke a word
And everything was calm again
For even nature heard.

They traveled on across the lake
And when they reached the shore,
They met a man who cried and screamed,
Tormented, sad, and sore.

But once again, the Savior spoke
To calm this inward storm,
And once set free, the troubled man
Grew calm, set free from harm.

The Light Within
October 25, Luke 10–11

Do you remember the children's song,
"This Little Light of Mine"?
Even the little children know that light is meant to shine.

That light is the love of Jesus, which guides us night and day,
And should be shared with everyone we meet along life's way.

Each time we chase the darkness by sharing God's sweet love,
The world's a little brighter and God smiles from above.

So let your light shine brightly—a beacon on a hill.
And with each service done for God
that light shines brighter still.

Oh, Jerusalem, Jerusalem
October 26, Luke 12–13

Oh Jerusalem, Jerusalem, how sadly rang His cry,
When Jesus knew the time was near
when He would have to die.

Oh, city of Jerusalem that sits upon a hill,
You talk about your love for God, but you don't seek His will.

Your fathers killed the prophets. You plan to do the same.
And yet you think you do it all in God's most holy name.

If only you had understood the love I have for you,
The shelter that I offer, and the gift of all I do.

I am the long-awaited One—God's sacrificial lamb;
Messiah, mighty Savior—I am the great I Am.

Count the Cost

October 27, Luke 14–16

When called upon to serve the Lord,
What answer do you give?
He never promised it would be
An easy way to live.

Jesus taught the people
To always count the cost.
For we must finish what we start
Or all will just be lost.

Jesus taught a story
Of a king who went to war.
If he had not prepared his troops
They wouldn't get too far.

Or if a man was building
A tower to his name,
But soon ran out of money,
His fame would turn to shame.

Salvation cost our Savior
His life upon the cross.
Make no mistake, a Christian life
Will still have pain and loss.

Sight to the Blind
October 28, Luke 17–18

I cannot imagine how much sadder life could be
Than to be a person who's born blind and never got to see.

Never to see a sunset or a storm cloud's darkened hue;
Never to gaze at the heavens where the sky is a clear, deep blue.

Never to see a flower or a blue jay on the wing;
Of all God's great creation—to never see a thing.

No wonder Christ showed mercy and
healed a man born blind.
Our vision is a treasure of the very richest kind.

Fickle Fans
October 29, Luke 19–20

As Jesus Christ came down the mount toward Jerusalem,
The people cried out words of joy to praise and honor Him.

They spread their cloaks upon the road
and blessed His holy name,
But Jesus knew it wouldn't last—this sudden, shallow fame.

For just a few days later, this same crowd turned around,
And cried out, "Crucify Him." It was a frightful sound.

Today we have our heroes in every kind of sport,
And when the team is winning, the fans give strong support.

But let a player falter or make a foolish call,
And suddenly the fans are fiends and show no love at all.

One Day Soon
October 30, Luke 21–22

Luke tells us that Jesus spoke of signs that we would see.
Signs in the sun, the moon, the stars, and in the tossing sea.

And when we see these signs, He said, that we were not to fear.
It meant that He was coming soon.
Redemption would be near.

I offer no prediction. Such knowledge is not mine.
But if you look around you, you just might see such signs.

People now have gone so far; they've walked upon the moon.
Could this be a simple sign that He is coming soon?

Weather patterns are so changed—it's either flood or drought.
And evil hearts bring death and pain of that there is no doubt.

So lift your eyes to heaven. He may not come today.
But one thing is for certain: He'll soon be on His way.

Times of Grief
October 31, Luke 23–24

While children sleep,
Their mothers weep
In fear for their tomorrow.
And women wept
Their vigil kept
As Christ endured His sorrow.

Lots were cast,
The morning passed,
As Christ was slowly dying.
The women there
Bowed down with care,
Watched painfully while crying.

Darkness fell
And all could tell
That nature too was weeping.
Then Christ called out
And with a shout
Placed His spirit in God's keeping.

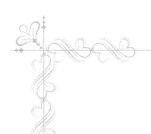

Teachings from John

November 1, John 1–3

There are many teachings
That man can't comprehend.
Like how God is forever,
No beginning and no end.

Another one that's difficult
Is that our God is one,
Although we clearly see Him
As a Father and His Son.

And then the Holy Spirit
Completes the Godhead three,
But I cannot explain it—
It is much too deep for me.

By faith I will accept them,
These things I cannot see.
God says them in His Holy Word,
That's good enough for me.

Right on Time
November 2, John 4–5

A man once came to Jesus to ask healing for his son.
Jesus sent him home again. He said the deed was done.

The man gave no resistance, no argument or plea.
He simply headed right back home
to see how things might be.

As he traveled homeward, his servants met him there
And told him that his son was fine. He needn't have a care.

He asked when this had happened. When did the fever leave?
And learned it was exactly when Christ told him to believe.

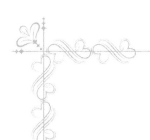

To Eat and Drink
November 3, John 6–8

What on earth did Jesus mean when people heard Him say,
Eat My flesh and drink My blood—there is no other way?

Now He was not referring to eating like a meal.
He meant to let Him in our lives, becoming strong and real.

It's a little bit like reading the Bible every day.
It soon becomes a part of you in all you do and say.

Just like in Revelation, John received a little scroll
That he was told to take and eat and it enriched his soul.

Much of Scripture's written in parables and such.
So we must read with open minds and
hearts tuned to His touch.

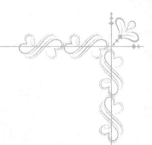

Jesus the Shepherd
November 4, John 9–10

Today folks live in cities stretching all across our land.
And when you speak of shepherds,
they don't really understand.

But Jesus is our Shepherd. He said it many times.
And only He can save us from sin's destructive grime.

A shepherd is a guardian who stands beside his sheep
And guards them from all danger while
they graze and while they sleep.

He offers them protection and calls each one by name.
And if we'll only follow Him, He offers us the same.

Head Knowledge
November 5, John 11–12

It's easy for us in a Sunday School class to
know the right answers to give.
We know that God wants us to love and to
care. We know how He wants us to live.

But having the knowledge within us and
knowing the right words to say
Does not always mean that living it out
is something we do every day.

Martha, the sister of Lazarus, had a
friendship with Jesus our Lord.
And when Lazarus died and was buried,
she took it extremely hard.

When Jesus asked her a question, she
said, "I know he will rise."
But in her heart there were questions of
what happens when somebody dies.

When Jesus approached the tombstone
and told them to roll it away
Martha spoke up quickly, "But, Lord, it has been four days."

So don't judge others too quickly.
Sometimes the things that we say
We know in our head are right answers,
but our heart doesn't always obey.

Fruit
November 6, John 13–16

Jesus told a story that some of us will find
Intriguing, for it tells about the branches of a vine.

I'm not much of a gardener, but I know Jesus said
A branch that doesn't produce fruit might just as well be dead.

Now even if a "little fruit" is all the gardener sees,
Then he will take and prune it so "more fruitful" it will be.

And finally He tells us if we walk beside the Lord,
Our lives will bear "much fruit" for
Him and great is our reward.

Truth

November 7, John 17–18

"What is truth?" Pilate asked. But he didn't want to know.
For if he did he'd have to pay for treating Jesus so.

Jesus taught, "I am the truth. I am the life, the way."
And if you want to come to God, I am the only way.

The truth is Jesus loves us and came to pay our way
That we might go to heaven to be with Him someday.

The truth is Jesus is a King and has been from the start.
But the kingdom that he cares about
is the kingdom of our heart.

The truth that Pilate questioned stood right before his face.
And if he'd only listened, he'd have learned of saving grace.

John the Beloved
November 8, John 19–21

Did you ever wonder why
Just before His final cry
Jesus placed His mother in John's care?
Surely there were others,
Such as His own brothers,
Who could have been called on to do their share.

Christ knew there was no other
Who would care so for His mother.
They called John the disciple Jesus loved.
And when John started writing,
His message was exciting.
He clearly knew that Christ came from above.

For John had walked beside Him
And he felt the Spirit guide Him.
He saw the many miracles Christ had done.
John's faith had grown unshakeable;
The power of love unbreakable.
Surely this could only be God's Son.

The Book of Acts

November 9, Acts 1–3

Luke was a medical doctor, and he was a Gentile as well.
He wrote two of the books in our Bible
for he had much to tell.

He told how eleven apostles, met for a time of prayer,
To replace Judas Iscariot and many followers were there.

They chose a man named Matthias, about
whom we don't know much,
Except that he came to be one of the twelve
chosen by God's own touch.

Then came the day of Pentecost, when the Holy Spirit came,
And brought them the very power of
God, appearing like tiny flames.

The book of Acts tells the story of how the church began—
A story that's still moving forward; we
must pass it on when we can.

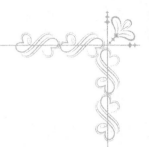

In This Name
November 10, Acts 4–6

Today we often choose a name on popularity.
But in the early Bible days, they stressed genealogy.

To speak a word in someone's name, suggested it was true
That you had their authority—that person stood by you.

That's why the Jewish leaders asked, "By
what power or name did you
Teach this way or bring about the things we see you do?"

Peter understood that, and many times he said,
"In the name of Jesus Christ," so folks were not misled.

He never claimed the power was his.
He never sought for glory.
And so he claimed that holy Name each time he told his story.

Short Stories
November 11, Acts 7–8

The book of Acts moves quickly as the church began to grow.
And there were many people whose stories we should know.

Stephen stood before the priest and gave the history
Of how God blessed His people and from Egypt set them free.

Then we meet a man named Saul, for he was standing by
To hold the coats of others as he watched while Stephen died.

Philip, sent by angels, met an Ethiopian man
And shared with him the Gospel—God's great salvation plan.

Then there was old Simon, who practiced sorcery,
Until he met Almighty God and changed his destiny.

Ananias

November 12, Acts 9–10

When we think of men of courage,
There's one name we can't leave out.
That man was Ananias
Who we don't know much about.

When Luke tells us his story,
We get a picture clear
Of how he sought to serve the Lord
In spite of doubt and fear.

Saul had a reputation
Which every Christian feared.
But he had met his Savior
As Damascus he had neared.

When God told Ananias
To minister to Paul,
He set aside his every fear
And answered Jesus's call.

An Excited Servant
November 13, Acts 11–13

An angel came to Peter as he sat in jail one night
To cast aside his shackles and free him from his plight.

Peter hurried forward, through streets as dark as sin,
And when he came to John Mark's
home, he knocked to enter in.

Now Rhoda was a servant, and when she heard his voice,
She ran to tell the others so they could all rejoice.

But she was so excited, she left him standing there,
Just outside the shelter of friends gathered there for prayer.

So Peter kept on knocking till they opened up the door,
Where he quickly told his story—God
had rescued him once more.

God's Math
November 14, Acts 14–16

You and I both learned in school that two times two is four.
But put God in that equation and you
may just get much more.

We all know the story of five little loaves of bread,
And how the hungry crowd of some
five thousand men was fed.

Now once when Paul and Barnabus were setting out to preach,
They had a disagreement and an answer could not reach.

So God just gently nudged them to go their separate ways,
And each one take a new teammate
to share their load each day.

And so we see it happen: when men would just divide,
With God in the equation, the workers multiplied.

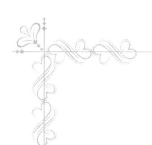

A Traveling Man
November 15, Acts 17–19

Paul was quite the traveler; he went from place to place
To share the Gospel message—the story of God's grace.

Many people listened, but there were some he found
Who didn't want to hear a word and
made him leave their town.

From Philippi to Berea to Athens by the sea,
In Corinth and in Ephesus, Paul spoke to set folks free.

The churches that he planted, it's plain for us to see,
Impacted all the then-known world and helped shape history.

Eutychus
November 16, Acts 20–22

Once, when Paul was preaching far into the night,
There were oil lamps burning to give a little light.

The heat and smoke brought drowsiness
to all within the room.
And one young man named Eutychus
fell three floors to his doom.

Paul threw his arms around him and quickly spoke a prayer,
And Eutychus stood to his feet and
joined those gathered there.

After Paul had taken time to eat a little bite,
He went back to his preaching until early morning light.

Paul then left for Assos where he would soon set sail,
Leaving Eutychus behind—his miracle to tell.

A Plot Revealed

November 17, Acts 23–25

As Paul, the great apostle, sat in his prison cell,
His nephew came to visit with quite a tale to tell.

It seems the boy had overheard a plot by evil men
To ambush Paul and bring his life and witness to an end.

Paul called to a centurion and asked that he would take
The boy to the commander for a statement he must make.

The boy told the commander the plot that he had heard,
And thanks to God, the man in charge believed his every word.

He called for two centurions with one hundred soldiers each.
He warned them of the dangers in a short and pointed speech.

And so the soldiers took him and safely he arrived.
The evil plot was thwarted and again Paul had survived.

Shipwreck Survivor
November 18, Acts 26–28

Paul gave such a testimony everywhere he went
That it should not surprise us how his prison days were spent.

First there was the shipwreck where everyone survived,
And then a viper bit him as soon as they arrived.

People watched and waited, expecting him to die.
Imagine their amazement—even sickness passed him by.

The people of the island brought their
sick who'd suffered much,
And God gave him the power to heal with just a gentle touch.

When Paul at last was taken to await his trial in Rome,
God saw that he was given his own small rented home.

For two whole years, he lived there. Imagine if you can
The many lives touched by the words of this dynamic man.

Paul Writes to Rome
November 19, Romans 1–3

The book of Romans comes to us courtesy of Paul.
He wrote it to explain to them about his faith and call.

He called himself a servant—an apostle set apart—
To share the Gospel message from a pure and caring heart.

He spoke to them of Jesus; God's holy, precious Son.
And pointed them to prophecies, which
proved He was the One.

Paul said that he was not ashamed, the Gospel to proclaim.
He wanted Jews and Gentiles both to know why Jesus came.

He warned them of unfaithfulness and sin of every kind,
And warned of Satan's strong desire to
tempt their heart and mind.

Paul Compares Wages to Gifts
November 20, Romans 4–7

Paul says when we receive a wage for labor we have done,
It shows that we have earned that pay,
though work may not be fun.

But there's no kind of labor that we can ever do
To earn our own salvation. It's a gift to me and you.

So when a gift is given, remember this the most,
There's only room for gratitude. There is no room to boast.

The thing we must remember is that even gifts aren't free.
Someone pays a price before they're given, don't you see.

Salvation is a gift from God through Jesus Christ, His Son.
And though an awful price He paid, it's free to anyone.

The Spirit Intercedes
November 21, Romans 8–10

When your heart is heavy laden and you really want to pray,
But the words are just not coming—
you just don't know what to say.
How wonderful it is to know the Spirit intercedes,
He knows and understands us all our sorrows and our needs.

He knows our every weakness. He knows just what to say
To keep us in the Father's will and guide us on our way.
So never be discouraged when words have let you down.
Be glad the Spirit's there to help. He'll turn your life around.

Living Sacrifice
November 22, Romans 11–13

What does Paul mean in his advice
To offer ourselves as a sacrifice?

It means you cannot always do
Just everything you wanted to.

If "everyone else" is doing it too,
That doesn't mean it is right for you.

When you do make the proper choice,
Don't speak of your act in a bragging voice.

Paul says our love must be sincere;
Our teaching should be plain and clear.

Be joyful in hope and faithful in prayer;
Living a life that shows you care.

Priscilla and Aquila
November 23, Romans 14–16

Priscilla and Aquila—what a precious, godly pair.
They worked to serve their Savior anytime and anywhere.

Paul spoke of them quite often, and always with a smile,
For they even lived and worked together for a little while.

When Paul sent out this letter to the Christians there in Rome,
He mentioned that the two of them
had church within their home.

Paul spoke of how they risked their lives, not just for him alone
But for all the Gentile churches where
the two of them were known.

They give us an example of the Christians we should be.
That we should always strive to offer hospitality.

Not With Eloquence
November 24, 1 Corinthians 1–4

Preachers today are often concerned
About preaching great sermons on lessons they've learned.

But Paul was a preacher with whom few compare,
And his style of preaching was forceful and rare.

He said that he came not with eloquent speech;
With no special wisdom had he come to preach.

The message was simple and perfect and true.
Christ laid down His life to save me and you.

Why clutter the matter with big fancy words?
Many that some of us never have heard.

Just tell us God loves us and sent His own Son.
Our debt has been paid and our victory won.

Passing Away
November 25, 1 Corinthians 5–9

Paul said life as we know it will someday pass away.
So we should not be too surprised by what we see today.

Polar bears are dying for loss of habitat.
Weather patterns changing—you can't argue with that.

The message Paul was giving—what he was trying to say—
Was don't invest your heart and soul in things that pass away.

This earthly life is fleeting. It won't last long at best.
So focus on eternity. Don't fret about the rest.

$\mathcal{L}ove$
November 26, 1 Corinthians 10–13

So you think that you're in love,
But true love comes from God above.
Listen to the words of Paul
And see if your love fits the call.

"Love is patient, love is kind."
Is that what you have in mind?
"Love does not envy." Can you say
That you truly feel that way?

"Love bears all things." That can be tough.
"Love always hopes" when times get rough.
Love "perseveres," that is to say
That you hang in there day by day.

No temper tantrums are allowed,
No voices raised to scream out loud.
True love will go the second mile
And still maintain a gentle smile.

Death and Resurrection
November 27, 1 Corinthians 14–16

Death is a doorway and nothing more
Through which we must step to reach Heaven's shore.
Christ led the way so we need not fear
For the promises He made are clear.

What kind of bodies will we have there?
They'll have a beauty beyond compare.
Picture a simple kernel of corn,
And the plant and the fruit that from it is born.

In the very same way, our bodies now
Will change and be glorified somehow.
Our resurrection is sure and true.
It's a promise Christ made to me and to you.

If you believe that Christ is God,
And on this earth as a human trod,
Then you must believe the things He said
About resurrection from the dead.

Jars of Clay
November 28, 2 Corinthians 1–4

Listen very carefully to what Paul had to say
When he compared us Christians to simple jars of clay.

A jar of clay is fragile, even at its best,
And often they are broken. They cannot stand the test.

Clay jars held great importance back then in Bible days
To carry water from the well and serve in other ways.

Mankind is just as fragile and prone to fall apart,
And yet God has entrusted us His message to impart.

The thing we must remember as we tell of God's great love
Is that our strength is not our own, it comes from God above.

On Layaway

November 29, 2 Corinthians 5-8

When I was raising children, and they were still quite small,
We didn't have much money to spend on gifts at all.

And so we used the layaway, that plan was just a must,
We paid a little money down and gifts were held in trust.

Now God has me on layaway; He's claimed me as His own.
And though I still live here on earth, I never am alone.

He gave the Holy Spirit as deposit till the day
When He'll come and redeem me and take me home to stay.

Masquerade
(To Transform or Disguise)
November 30, 2 Corinthians 9-13

Paul wrote to the Corinthians to warn of Satan's power.
He wanted them to be alert through every single hour.

He spoke of false apostles and those who work deceit.
He warned how they would masquerade
then turn and bring defeat.

He said this shouldn't take us completely by surprise,
For Satan set the pattern for wearing a disguise.

If Satan can transform himself as an angel of the light,
It's no big deal his ministers can make themselves look right.

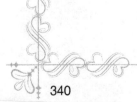

Abraham's Seed

December 1, Galatians 1–3

Paul said if we belong to Christ, we're seed of Abraham,
To whom God gave the promise of the sacrificial Lamb.

We cannot keep the law of God, no matter how we try.
God knew that, so in His plan, Christ came to earth to die.

The blood of Christ was worthy, for He is God's precious Son.
And that blood washed down every
wall and made all people one.

There is no male or female; there is no Jew or Greek.
There's only those who come to God in faith, His love to seek.

Abraham was saved by faith. He took God at His Word.
And you and I are saved by faith in the message we have heard.

Fruit of the Spirit
December 2, Galatians 4–6

The fruit of the Spirit is love, joy, and peace;
we all want a nature like that.
But Paul didn't stop with only those three.
There are several more named after that.

There is kindness and goodness and gentleness too.
Are we faithful in living those three?
Sometimes it is hard to live every day as
the people that we ought to be.

And what about patience? Boy!
That one is tough because we like to be in control.
We want what we want and we don't like to wait,
But patience should still be our goal.

Then there is faithfulness,
Where we stand strong in spite of the storm winds which blow.
But fruit doesn't grow unless nurtured and
fed, so back to the Savior we go.

For this is fruit of the Spirit, Paul says. We
can't live like that on our own.
But with Christ in control and submission our goal,
It's the best life mankind's ever known.

A Positive Influence
December 3, Ephesians 1–3

Folks who say the Bible is nothing but a book
Filled with lots of "thou shall nots" should take another look.

Read the little letter that Paul wrote long ago
To the church of the Ephesians to help them learn and grow.

Paul tells us how God loves us and adopted us as sons.
We have redemption through Christ's
blood. We are the blessed ones.

He speaks of our forgiveness and the riches of God's grace,
And all because Christ paid the price by dying in our place.

Paul wrote this while in prison, but that didn't get him down.
So let his courage speak to you and turn your life around.

Imitators of God
December 4, Ephesians 4–6

First we looked at the positive side as
written by Paul in this letter.
Now he describes the things to avoid if
we want to make ourselves better.

He warns against all immorality and every type of greed.
Coarse joking and obscenity—a Christian does not need.

If you study what is written, storing God's Word in your heart,
You'll recognize the empty words so many folks impart.

Reach out a hand to others. Be generous to give.
As Paul wrote to God's people, "Be careful how you live."

Paul's Prayer

December 5, Philippians 1–4

Paul always wrote his letters
With words of hope and love.
He wanted folks to live their lives
In praise to God above.

He prayed for understanding
And insight as they grew,
And strength to live for God each day
And keep their witness true.

He prayed they would be blameless—
Their love and service pure.
Christ soon would come and take them home,
Till then they must endure.

Devote Yourselves to Prayer
December 6, Colossians 1–4

Christ gave to His disciples, a simple model prayer.
And Paul wrote in his letters, we should pray for other's cares.

He wrote we should be watchful over those we live around;
Always being thankful for the love and joy we've found.

Paul wrote this letter long go, and yet it speaks today
To this thanksgiving season as we take more time to pray.

We're thankful to the Father and to those who've gone before,
But don't forget the folks who live just outside your door.

Pray for their well-being, their safety, and their goals.
But also pray a prayer of thanks for friends both new and old.

May Your Love Increase
December 7, 1 Thessalonians 1–5

We can learn so much from Paul in the way we hear him pray.
I wonder just how often we're inclined to pray that way.

He told the Thessalonians he prayed God would increase
Their love for one another and that it would never cease.

He asked that God would strengthen
their hearts beyond degree,
That they might be found blameless when they faced eternity.

We pray for those with illnesses and
grief which weighs them down.
But a prayer that their love might
increase—I doubt that's ever found.

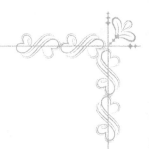

Stay Busy
December 8, 2 Thessalonians 1–3

Paul wrote the Thessalonians a message strong and clear.
Don't believe the rumors and false teachings that you hear.

He told them persecutions were trials they must endure.
But someday God would settle things
with judgment right and pure.

Meanwhile, they must stay busy; their work was not yet done
To share the gospel message of salvation through God's Son.

Don't waste your time on theories as
to when Christ will return.
Just serve each day with gladness and
His pleasure you will earn.

Letter to a Young Pastor
December 9, 1 Timothy 1–6

Paul wrote to young Timothy words of good advice
To guard against false teachers or the
church would pay the price.

Paul taught him to be loving and treat folks with respect.
He spoke of Christian conduct he must teach and not neglect.

He spoke of how true beauty should come from deep within.
And Paul reminded Timothy that pride was Satan's sin.

Three times Paul told young Timothy
the words he spoke were true.
And Timothy could trust in them to always see him through.

With words like *mercy*, *love*, and *grace*, he drew a picture clear
Of our great God, the only God, who wants us to draw near.

Words of Encouragement
December 10, 2 Timothy 1–4

Paul wrote again to Timothy
And spoke of his great love.
His constant prayers for Timothy
As he served God above.

Paul wrote this while in prison,
Yet he did not complain.
He knew his death was imminent,
But he saw that as gain.

So all his words to Timothy
Encouraged him to preach—
To always speak with strength and love,
Meant to guide and teach.

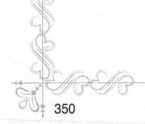

Guidelines
December 11 (Part 1), Titus 1–3

Titus was a young man who served with love and care,
And Paul asked him to stay in Crete to teach the people there.

Paul gave him clear instructions of how the church should be,
And if we study them today, their wisdom we can see.

We need to work together in loving harmony
That we might show a sinful world how great a life can be.

Philemon
December 11 (Part 2), Philemon 1

Paul wrote this little letter to Philemon to say
He knew about Onesimus—the slave who ran away.

But Paul had led him to the Lord and
knew that he had changed.
And so he sent Philemon a request that might seem strange.

Paul urged him to accept him back, no longer as a slave
But as a Christian brother, whom he welcomed and forgave.

Greater Than
December 12, Hebrews 1–4

Hebrews tells us plainly of superiority,
Of Jesus over angels for the Son of God is He.
Angels are God's messengers, but servants all the same.
Jesus is far greater as we see by just His name.

Moses was a man of God and held in high regard.
But Jesus is far greater, for Jesus is our Lord.
Moses led the people as good preachers do today,
But still they're only human and will someday pass away.

Jesus is far greater than the priests who stood back then
To intercede for people for forgiveness of their sin.
But Jesus faced temptation, the same as you and me,
Yet He was always perfect. He lived His life sin free.

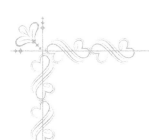

Melchizedek
December 13, Hebrews 5–7

The story of Melchizedek—in Hebrews it is told—
Is quite an illustration as we see how it unfolds.

His name means "king of righteousness."
He served God as a priest.
And Abraham paid tithes to him, the greater to the least.

He was the "king of Salem," which means the king of "peace."
And he was told his priesthood would never, ever cease.

It's really quite a story, although hard to understand.
His priesthood is compared to Christ—the only perfect man.

The New Covenant

December 14, Hebrews 8–10

The original covenant given to man
Was meant to point to salvation's plan.
With words like *shadow* and *copy*, we see
One day a better plan there would be.

No matter how many animals died,
Our guilt and sin we could not hide.
Yet the Lamb of God brought the gift of grace
When He gave His life to take our place.

The curtain which tore in the temple that day,
Like the flesh of Christ, it opened the way.
We no longer need another man
To stand between us and salvation's plan.

I'm so grateful to God above,
For a covenant built on His pure love.
The gift of grace, it seems to me,
Is the greatest covenant there can be.

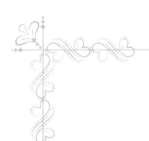

Reverence and Awe
December 15, Hebrews 11–13

Today within our churches, we are taught things should be big.
Clap your hands and lift your voice and dance a little jig.
But there's a certain passage in our Scripture for today
That speaks of worship service in a very different way.

The writer to the Hebrews spoke of faith and love and law.
He uses words like *reverence* and *Godly fear* or *awe*.
Why don't leaders understand? It really isn't hard.
How can dancing in the aisles show reverence for our Lord?

Even Moses stood barefoot, his shoes he had cast down.
God told him to remove them for he stood on Holy ground.
If, in a barren desert, we owe God our respect,
How much more within His house do you think He expects?

Faith in Action

December 16, James 1–5

A testimony given by word of mouth is good.
But does the life you're living reflect Christ as it should?

If someone shares a prayer request for you to intercede,
Do you try hard to find a way to help to meet that need?

Abraham believed God and offered up his son.
His faith was put in action to see the deed was done.

Rahab proved her faith was strong
when spies came to her door.
She hid them and it brought to her salvation and much more.

So even though the deeds we do won't earn eternity,
Faith in action shows the world our hope and destiny.

Living Hope
December 17, 1 Peter 1–2

Peter writes to people
Whose sufferings are great.
And gently he reminds them
Of their destiny and fate.

Jesus paid our penalty
Upon a cruel tree.
But three days later, He arose.
From death He was set free.

Now you and I, as Christians,
Live in this hope each day.
He died for us—He lives for us—
He'll keep us all the way.

That hope is the foundation
On which we live our lives.
And even when we face tough times,
Our courage grows and thrives.

Submission
December 18, 1 Peter 3–5

Submission is a funny word and how we turn away.
Because we do not understand just what it has to say.

Most folks don't understand it. They fear it means to be
No better than a doormat—dumb as dirt as all can see.

But that is not the meaning. It's not what you expect.
Submission is to yield yourself in love and in respect.

Christ, Himself, submitted to death upon the cross.
If our submission wins a soul, how can that be a loss?

Knowledge of God
December 19, 2 Peter 1–3

Why do I take time to read my Bible every day?
Just read this little letter. See what Peter had to say.

He warns us of false teachers and the damage they can do.
It's only as we know God's Word that we can remain true.

He tells us to seek knowledge and to always be on guard,
For life is filled with twists and turns
and sometimes gets real hard.

But as we read the Scripture, the more our hearts will grow,
And as we seek to follow Christ, our faithfulness will show.

John's Words
December 20, 1 John 1–3

John was growing older when he took pen in hand
To write this little letter and help folks understand.

After all, the stories that John set out to share,
Were stories he had witnessed—he knew for he was there.

He used strong words of contrast to make the lessons clear.
He spoke of light and darkness, of confidence and fear.

He spoke of strong emotions—of godly love and hate.
His words are clear and simple and never out of date.

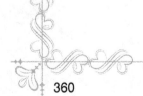

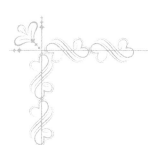

Test the Spirits
December 21, 1 John 4–5

There was a time in history, at least there was for me,
I thought words I saw written down were true as true could be.

Sadly, through the years I've learned that simply isn't true,
And so we must be careful of the words we listen to.

John tells us, "Test the Spirits." His words are very clear.
We mustn't follow after every doctrine that we hear.

If someone tries to tell you the Bible's just a book,
My friend, you'd better take the time to have a second look.

Jesus wasn't "just a man" as some folks try to say.
So let His Word speak truth to you, and always, always pray.

Walk in Love
December 22 (Part 1), 2 John

John writes this simple message that they should walk in love,
And wishes them both grace and peace, obeying God above.

Gaius
December 22 (Part 2), 3 John

John wrote to his friend Gaius to tell him that he knew
That Gaius opened heart and home
to brothers passing through.

Jesus's Brother
December 22 (Part 3), Jude

Jude was Jesus's brother, and once he understood
That Jesus was Messiah, he served every way he could.

Christ Revealed
December 23, Revelation 1–2

Lord, I'm trying hard to understand what I just read.
I know that when John wrote it, his words were Spirit led.
But Lord, we know so little, in our modern world today,
Of lamp stands and of angels that you send to guide our way.

But this I know for certain: Your word is crystal clear.
Since I've been washed in Jesus's blood, I have no need to fear.
I may go through some battles, but this much I do know,
God above is sovereign and He will not let me go.

Letters to the Churches
December 24, Revelation 3–5

The letters John was told to write to churches long ago
Speak just as much to us today, and they were meant to show
Encouragement for things done right,
strong warnings against wrong,
And how our faithful service should give us a brand-new song.

Then God gave John a vision of heaven's open door.
He let him see His holy throne, a rainbow, and much more.
It must have been so hard for John to even find the words
To help his readers understand the things he saw and heard.

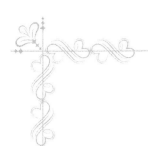

Four Horsemen
December 25, Revelation 6–8

As John wrote down his vision so many years ago,
He used a lot of symbols whose meanings we don't know.

He spoke about four horses, each colored differently,
And folks have wondered through the
years what each is meant to be.

John speaks of seven trumpets and of seven seals as well,
Each with a special message that God wants them to tell.

Although these are word pictures which we don't understand,
One thing that we can know for sure: our God is in command.

No More Delay

December 26, Revelation 9–11

John saw a "mighty angel" from heaven coming down.
He placed his right foot on the sea, his left foot on the ground.

He raised his hand to heaven, and then John heard him say,
God's mystery will be revealed, there'll be no more delay.

The voice of seven thunders responded to the sound
And told John he must seal it up and must not write it down.

Again, the message that we see is God has all the power.
He controls the judgments and He knows the final hour.

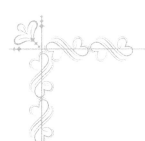

In Bethlehem That Night

December 27, Revelation 12–13

Oh, little town of Bethlehem, in you such war was waged.
For when God's precious Son was born, the evil Satan raged.

We all have heard the story: how the angels came that night
And gave a group of shepherds a sudden, wondrous fright.

But here in Revelation, John tells another tale
Of how the evil Satan fought, but Michael did prevail.

Things weren't so quiet in Bethlehem that night so long ago.
A mighty war was raging. People simply didn't know.

Seven Bowl Judgments
December 28, Revelation 14–16

The seven bowls of God's great wrath we read about today
Bring to mind the plagues God sent way back in Moses day.

A plague which caused a breaking out
of great and painful sores;
A plague which turned the sea to blood
and dead fish washed ashore.

Another caused the rivers and the springs to bleed as well,
And then the sun was given power to burn as hot as hell.

The fifth one caused a dreadful dark upon the evil one.
And still the people would not turn
from all that they had done.

The sixth plague dried the river which
had been a strong defense,
And people still would not repent—it simply makes no sense.

The final bowl of judgment was a voice which said, "It's done."
And when an earthquake rent the earth,
men had nowhere to run.

Woe to Babylon
December 29, Revelation 17–18

With a series of three sets of woe!
John tells us how Babylon will go.
He says she's a home
For the demons that roam
And the grief that the merchants will show.

He speaks of the wealth she once knew.
But evil and greed quickly grew.
Then one day at last,
Her glory will pass,
And she'll crumble and fade from view.

Babylon is only a name
For a lifestyle of sin and of shame.
We need to stay true
In the things that we do,
Or our future will turn out the same.

A Place Called Hell

December 30, Revelation 19–20

Do you believe in hell, my friend? Not many people do.
If they did, they wouldn't live the thoughtless way they do.

John was quite specific. His words are strong and true.
He tells us of a lake of fire with no relief in view.

It was designed for Satan and sin and death as well.
And we have come to know it as the punishment called hell.

But don't miss John's sharp warning.
Unless your name is found
Written in the Book of Life, for hell you too are bound.

A place of separation, no more to see God's face.
You surely do not want to go to such a dreadful place.

The Beginning and the End

December 31, Revelation 21–22

Now we have taken quite a look
At every page of this great book.
A book of stories we've been told,
Handed down from men of old.

Life started in a garden fair,
And God walked with His children there.
But then old Satan slithered in
And drew God's children into sin.

All through the years of history,
God worked to show His mystery
Of how He loved us each so much
He sent His Son—each life to touch.

In Revelation, John has shown
That God still rules upon His throne.
And one day soon, the devil's hour
Will reach its end—he'll lose his power.

Christ was there to start it all,
And He has caused the devil's fall.
One day, a new earth we will see,
Where we will live eternally.

About the Author

Frances Henderson has lived in Houston all her life. Her favorite role in life has been that of mother. She is a biological mother, a stepmother, a grandmother, and a great-grandmother. She has also served as room mother, den mother, and foster mother. Frances has been writing poetry as long as she can remember. She began studying the Bible as a very young girl at her grandmother's side and has taught Bible study for many years now. This book is a blending of those two loves—poetry and Bible study. She is grateful for the love and encouragement of her beloved husband, now with the Lord, and her granddaughter who helped make it ready for publication.